The
Reformation

The
Reformation

THIRD EDITION

. . .

George L. Mosse

University of Wisconsin

THE DRYDEN PRESS INC.
HINSDALE, ILLINOIS

Preface

A prominent historian once wrote that "what man is, only history tells." This is certainly true if we want to understand the evolution of man in the society that he has made for himself. The age of the Reformation represents a crucial step in that historical development. Through their own thought the reformers mirrored the doubts, hopes, and aspirations of the people of Europe. Yet it has been difficult to find modern interpretations of the age which are neither too specialized nor too elementary. Such interpretations undoubtedly do exist, but in the form of larger and more detailed analyses or as chapters in general works. This book is meant to provide an initial grasp of this epoch, and the Bibliographical Note at the end of the work will enable those so inclined to go further into the problems and interpretations of the age.

To an older generation of historians it seemed sufficient to "present all the facts and let them speak for themselves." Today we realize that historical analysis is a more complex business; facts are only meaningful when they have been subjected to the historian's skill of interpretation. This book attempts an interpretation of the Reformation's crowded history. Until recently such interpretations were akin to those polemics which filled the sixteenth century; old religious enmities prevented a more judicious examination of this period. Such a state of affairs is happily receding into the past, and the areas of agreement among Catholic and Protestant historians have become ever larger. As a result, there is hardly another area of modern scholarship in which there has been so general a revaluation. It is hoped that this book reflects the advances of such scholarship.

This study centers upon the religious scene itself. Unless this is properly understood, the social, political, and economic factors of the age will seem inexplicable. The link between life and thought is indissoluble, but during the Reformation, at least, the elucidation of the thought is of prime importance for an understanding of the life of the period. It has also been necessary to emphasize the Protestant rather than the Catholic reformation. Within the brief compass of this introduction, such a choice seemed warranted in order to give some depth to the ideas and events discussed.

Madison, Wisconsin   G. L. M.
January 1963

Acknowledgment

Any summary of so vast a period of history must rely upon specialized works in the field. As there are no notes to the text, I must express my gratitude in this manner to those scholars whose recent works have been especially useful to me: Roland H. Bainton, Pierre Janelle, Hubert Jedin, Thomas Parker, and Francois Wendell. For the many other works upon which I have relied a general acknowledgment must suffice. I am grateful to my former colleagues Ralph Greenlaw and Philip A. M. Taylor for their close reading of the manuscript. The late Professor Laurence Packard of Amherst College provided valuable editorial advice. The services of Robert E. Ruigh, William Lucht, Morton Rosenberg, Carl Weiner, and Burton Pines in preparing this work for publication were much appreciated.

Contents

CHAPTER . . . 1

Why It Happened

Why did the Reformation happen? Why did a religious cataclysm at the beginning of the sixteenth century put an end to the medieval *Respublica Christiana* and in so doing usher in the modern age at an accelerated pace? Such rapid changes in history usually come about when the gulf between what is and what should be, between outward reality and the human condition, becomes painfully apparent. At that point a leader can spark an attempt to bring to an end the dilemma created by such a situation. Luther was such a leader and he as well as the other reformers found Europe prepared for their message. This was something new. There had been attempted reformations throughout the Middle Ages, but they had all failed where the Reformation of the sixteenth century succeeded.

The success of the Reformation climaxed several centuries during which some men had unsuccessfully tried to cope with the changing relationships between political and economic power, between the professed aims of Christianity and the visible reality of the Church. To analyze some of these changes in relationships is to illustrate the basic causes of the Reformation itself. Though this Reformation was a religious movement, centered on a concern for salvation, it nevertheless wrote its message upon a canvass much wider than this. If men expressed their dilemmas in religious terminology and through religious longings it was because this was their ideology: they saw their entire way of life and attitude toward life in the terms of Christianity. Any change in religion meant a change in the whole tenor of life itself.

The shift in political power which sought expression was one away from any universalism toward territorially limited political units. Nationalism was not unknown in the Middle Ages and throughout the later part of that age the nation-state, principality, or free city emerged as the important repositories of political power. In opposition were the claims of papal imperialism which had been asserted with increasing urgency ever since Pope Innocent III. The individual rulers of Europe opposed this imperialism with increasing success. But the papacy did not relinquish its claims for political power and this led, in the end, to a period of papal captivity in France which was to mean a split in the papacy itself. Even then each of the rival popes continued to claim great powers which were totally contradicted by the realities of their own situation. The papacy was caught in a general shift of political power. Though it had dealt more or less successfully with the claims of the Hohenstauffen emperors, it could not do so with those of the territorial rulers who possessed in their domains an actual power with which the pope could not cope; his claims seemed far removed from the realities of a changing Europe.

Thus there emerged an area of political tension between what was asserted on behalf of the Church and a new situation which was the actual reality. A second element of conflict arose through the economic policies of the Church. The taxes imposed, the tributes taken, made increasingly apparent a difference between what was and what should be in terms of the Christian profession of faith. If Christ had been poor and had preached poverty, why should the Church be so rich? Monastic orders had always stood for such an ideal of poverty. The Franciscans exemplified this ideal in the later Middle Ages for they put increasing stress upon the necessity for poverty when other orders were falling away from the monastic ideal. It is typical of the conflict between the concept of a "poor Church" and the papal actuality that this emphasis brought the Franciscans into a bitter conflict with the pope. John XXII declared them heretical (1317) and asserted that Christ and the Apostles had never possessed common property. Most of the order submitted, but the papacy had now clearly committed itself not only to continue its financial policies but also to a rejection of what many held to be the "true" Church of Christ.

The political claims of the papacy were accompanied by an outward pomp and glory which gave them symbolical expression. It was the economic exactions of the pope which seemed to make his worldly magnificence possible. Accusations of luxury and avarice were leveled against the papacy throughout the Middle Ages. All of this removed the church organization from contact with the people and with the parish clergy as well, who in consequence did little to resist the Reformation. John Wycliffe wrote (1378) that even if the pope should be predestined to be the head of the Church, he is still only second in command under Christ. Yet the papacy seemed to behave and to act as if the incumbent of the throne of St. Peter was the sole shepherd of the faithful and their absolute overlord. He attempted to enforce his far-reaching claims, he took tribute and taxes to keep up a court more worldly than spiritual, and he seemed to have forgotten that Christ had preached poverty and humility. This was important precisely because the people themselves did care about the Church.

Europe before the Reformation saw a religious revival which we will discuss in more detail under heading of Popular Piety. Not only the common people but the intellectuals as well had a deep concern about the state of the Church. We must always remember that, to medieval man, the problems of daily life were argued out in religious terms and that the modern fissure between religion and life had not yet come about. The tension between a papacy as it should be and as it was, exhorbitant yet impotent, led to a questioning of the whole religious system upon which it was built. Indeed, the system itself no longer seemed to many men in tune with the changing times.

The hierarchical system advocated by the Church was symbolized not only by its actual organizational structure but also by the whole edifice of Catholic religious thought. Both were being challenged. As the world itself was ordered to the final and transcendent end, so, within the world, all was ordered in a proper hierarchical structure with a view to that end. But no matter how organic this system was (as explained by St. Thomas Aquinas) the individual parts of this structure tended to fall asunder, to recall their own purposes. Whether in political terms—princes against the emperor and pope—or in terms of the religious system, individualism was from the first a severe challenge to this whole edifice. On the eve of the Reformation this individualism had made inroads among intellectuals through both Platonic and Aristotelian ideas coming from Italy. That man himself, outside any ordered hierarchy, could be the reflection of the Divine was the crux of such thought. Among the common people mysticism provided a similar release from this hierarchical system: each human could attain, for a moment at least, contact with God himself.

This individualism, however, was not that of the

liberalism of the nineteenth century. It centered on establishing contact with God or upon understanding the classical authors and did not readily penetrate the political or economic realm. It was a religious rather than a secular individualism, an important distinction. Historians have often made Luther the founder of liberalism through stressing the individualistic implications in his faith. But he himself believed in a Christian "community" and indeed the reformers tended to revitalize the concept of the community rather than that of a political or social individualism. This is a point to which we shall return in the conclusion for it is of some importance in correctly assessing what the reformers wanted to accomplish. The individualism which challenged the hierarchical system of the established Church was a liberty of the spirit rather than a liberty of the flesh, to use the terminology of the times. It is true, though, that once this liberty had established itself, the lower classes of the population could and did translate it into social and economic terms.

This individualism little required a clergy to mediate between God and man. It tended to bypass a church organization which had lost touch with many of the faithful and which was, in their minds, getting ever further away from true Christianity. Joseph Lortz has called the Reformation a lay revolt against the papacy. The laity, long before the actual events of the Reformation, was imbued with skepticism toward both papal claims and a religious system which seemed contrary to man's capabilities. Men for whom religion meant a way of life were crying out to have the increasing tensions within it resolved.

Life was becoming ever more complex and confusing in a society which attempted to rationalize its economic processes as it passed from an agricultural into a commercial age. Peasants found themselves economically hard pressed without knowing why this should be so; the bourgeois in the towns felt a new self-confidence as commercial activity accelerated. A working class made up of men who had no chance to rise in the social scale was slowly coming into being. Warrior knights were becoming obsolete as rulers attempted to fasten a centralized administrative system upon feudal Europe. All these changes were bound to express themselves in a cumulative fashion, and they did so through a sharpening of the religious dilemma. Added to these factors was the periodic and severe outbreak of the plague, which decimated the regions where it did its worst. Given the ever more apparent gulf between what the Church claimed to be and what it was, religious disorientation was a response to an age of natural catastrophes and heightened change. The impetus of popular piety was escaping the confines of church organization. A link had to be forged between Christianity and those realities which impinged upon many people and which these people felt should determine the task of the Church.

These basic factors aided Luther in his task and helped to make him successful where so many others had failed. Above all, they sustained the momentum of what he was trying to accomplish, for the Reformation was in its beginnings no sudden revolution. This was true for Luther himself and for wide circles of his followers who had no idea of the far-reaching consequences of his theological opposition to some church practices. To be sure, the Reformation took place within a single generation, from roughly 1517 when Luther posted his famous theses against indulgences in Wittenberg to 1555 when Calvin became firmly established. But the start was slow, and not until 1521 did the break with Rome become obvious. Attempts at reconciliation were made as late as 1541. There was no storming of a Bastille to symbolize a revolution, no well-organized revolutionary councils to put down the opposition. The Reformation unfolded, and only as it did so did its implications become clear. No break with the past was intended, the opposition to the Church couched its demands in terms of conservatism. Historical connections were always sought; the plea was for a return to a time when Christianity had been "true" and fulfilled its mission. Such efforts climaxed in the Magdeburger Zenturien (1559–1574), a Lutheran history of the Church divided by centuries (hence the title), which, on the basis of sources, attempted to show that the papacy departed from original Christianity and that Luther had forged that connection once again. The radicals of the Reformation shared that same appeal to the "good old times" in the far past.

The appeal to a continuity with the true past was a natural reaction to the bewildering changes with which the Church seemed to have lost contact. But this emphasis on the past helped to produce important changes which pointed to the future. Its main result was to slow down the actual rate of change. This decrease in tempo performed a service for the Reformation, for it set the new down side by side with the old. Luther changed the nature of the Mass but in a way not at first so readily apparent in the liturgy, and he kept the confessional intact. Those reformers who came after his pioneering days made more radical changes which, in this way, had been prepared already. It is this rhythm in the process of the reform which makes it quite different from modern revolutionary change in spite of such spectacular gestures as Luther's burning of the papal bull. Yet, in the end result, it did transform Europe and it did open the door to much that we consider modern rather than medieval.

But these changes, indeed the whole history of the Reformation, can only be understood within the religious context which generated and determined its course. It was a medieval revolt in as much as the question of faith dominated the social and political issues which cried for solution; indeed it rode roughshod over the political interests of some of its supporters. Salvation was all important and true Christianity would mean the end to those tensions we have dis-

cussed. In our more pragmatic age this seems difficult
to understand, but the key role of what we now call
ideology for men of the sixteenth century can not be
underrated. The Reformation was modern in as much
as it did produce a cataclysm which destroyed the
Respublica Christiana of the Middle Ages, both in
fact and in thought. But it did this always in the
name of constructing a more meaningful Christian
republic in its place.

CHAPTER . . . 2

Martin Luther

The Crises of the Papacy. The Reformation was a religious movement. Whatever far-reaching consequence
it was to have for our civilization, its primary concern
was with men's souls. The great reformers did not
question the primacy of the spiritual power over the
temporal; like medieval men in general, they were interested in the long-range goal of salvation rather than
in short-range efforts at improving life on earth. Only
from this point of view can we understand the soul
searching of Martin Luther or the unbending sense of
righteousness of John Calvin. The reformers were concerned with the Church rather than with the State,
and the profound political and social consequences of
their actions were important to them only insofar as
they furthered God's purpose. If in our wider historical perspective we see the Reformation as the last and
decisive crisis of the medieval *Respublica Christiana*,
such a viewpoint would have been repudiated by the
reformers themselves. They came to fulfill, not to de-

stroy; they thought of themselves as reformers, not as revolutionaries.\Martin Luther was most reluctant to break with established ecclesiastical forms, and it took him almost a decade to become reconciled to the consequences of his actions. The reformers of the second generation, men like Calvin and Zwingli, had Luther's example before them to make the break with the Church a little easier. But they, too, considered themselves conservatives, attached to political authority, wanting but to restore the Church to its ancient purity. These men became revolutionaries only when obliged to cut through the resistance which they encountered in their mission to save man and to serve God, whose plan for the universe they thought they understood. To comprehend how the quest for reform could result in a break with the medieval Church, it is necessary to analyze that Church on the eve of the Reformation more carefully than has been previously done. Here the condition of the papacy was of paramount importance, for the Church was like a monarchy in which the pope acted as the monarch.

By the time Martin Luther emerged from his monastery into the light of public controversy, the medieval papacy had already passed through several crises. The first severe blow to the Church had come around the year 1300 as a result of the claims to universal domination put forward by the pope. Temporal rulers were not prepared to tolerate the attempts of Pope Boniface VIII (1294–1303) to extend his influence. The papacy and the empire had engaged in a running struggle for power throughout the Middle Ages, but now the new national monarchies took a hand. It was France, the strongest of these monarchies, that won the immediate victory over the pope. For seventy-two years (1305–1377), the papacy was held captive at Avignon in the French kingdom. But worse was to follow; a second crisis threatened the already shaken foundations of the papal monarchy. A disputed succession to the papal throne (1378) produced two popes, one residing at

Martin Luther. (*The Granger Collection*)

Avignon and the other at Rome. All Europe took sides, according to national rather than religious interests. Nevertheless, Christendom was shocked by this evident weakness in the hierarchical structure of the Church. Among the profoundly pious common people, unswayed by dynastic or national interests, the demand for reform became vocal, strengthened by the general social unrest of the times. This demand expressed itself in many ways, the most dangerous of which, from the Church's point of view, were the heresies of Wycliffe in England and of Hus in Bohemia. Both came close to the view that no earthly church was needed for salvation, that faith and the Bible were the chief aids to the attainment of life hereafter. The immediate answer to the declining prestige of the papacy, however, was not heresy but the conciliar movement.

Intellectuals, clerics, and rulers began to see the dangers inherent in the chaotic religious situation, and the emperor assumed European leadership by calling for councils from all Christendom to put the affairs of the Church in order and to undertake the necessary reforms. Such councils met in Pisa (1409), in Constance (1414), and in Basel (1431). At Constance, where the most important of these councils met, the unity of the papacy was restored, but the stumbling block to effective action proved to be reform of the Church. Here, in spite of valiant attempts, failure resulted, since the pope himself worked actively against the authority of the councils once the unity of the papacy had been restored.

He was justified, for the action of these councils amounted to a vote of no confidence in the idea of papal supremacy over the Church. They attempted to introduce limitations on papal power such as parliaments exercised over kings in some of the Western nations. Writers stressed the idea that the Church, founded by Christ himself, could not deviate from her path or commit crimes, but popes and cardinals were quite capable of earthly corruption. For the conciliar theorists this was confirmed by the history of the popes, several of whom had been accused of heresy, and the behavior of the recent incumbents of the throne of St. Peter.

Nevertheless, the papacy succeeded once more in restoring the papal monarchy, buying off national rulers with concessions in financial exactions and ecclesiastical appointments, as well as playing off one ruler against the other. It was a reinvigorated papacy which emerged from this crisis; yet the conciliar idea was never to vanish from men's minds. The superiority of the "common corps of Christendom" over ecclesiastical institutions remained an ideal which could be appealed to by the reformers and which would find an echo in the hearts of many pious Christians. For the cause of church reform, which had been one of the chief reasons for the calling of the councils, never ceased to be an issue; and the papacy, reinvigorated though it was as an institution, did nothing to fulfill the hopes raised by the conciliar movement.

By the time Martin Luther called for the discussion of indulgences, the papacy seemed to have forgotten the crises through which it had passed. In these same years (1512–1517) the papacy, for the first time since the thirteenth century, felt itself strong enough to call together under its own auspices a council of Christendom. The Fifth Lateran Council received representatives from all over Europe. Even a bishop from San Domingo put in an appearance, symbolizing the extension of papal power over the new world. As its final act, the council reaffirmed the Bull *Unam Sanctam,* a most extreme statement of papal power dating from the pontificate of Boniface VIII. What did the pronouncements of a German monk amount to against such might? Yet, for all the splendor of the Lateran Council, there were several issues in church government which needed immediate reform; the outcome of the failure to resolve these was to nullify the triumph of the papacy over schism and councils. The severest and

most decisive crisis of papal power was yet to come—
the Reformation.

The Need for Reform. The need for reform was great
and especially urgent in the case of papal finance. Yet
here the papacy's hands were tied, for it faced the same
economic problems as the national monarchies. The
pope could not live "of his own"; the traditional
revenues no longer sufficed for the increased costs of
papal administration or for the maintenance of the
most splendid court in Europe. Hard pressed, the
papacy began to use the same expedient as lay rulers,
the sale of offices, which when applied to positions in
the Church was known as "simony." Not only clerics
but laymen as well benefited from this practice. Nor
did the papacy shy away from trafficking in indulgences,
an activity which came to symbolize the alliance between the Church and the monied interests.

Originally an indulgence was a relaxing of the
punishment (penance) imposed by the Church for
transgression against some religious commandment. At
first such indulgences were conferred upon those who
risked their lives in fighting against the infidel. Gradually, however, such active service for the common good
of Christendom was extended to include financial gifts
for worthy spiritual causes, even if the donor did not
actively participate in them. Thus financial sacrifice was
put on a level with the risk and sacrifice of one's life
for Christ's sake. The financing of cathedrals, monasteries, and hospitals was at times designated by the papacy
as warranting indulgence. Territorial rulers benefited,
for their support of an indulgence sold in their domain
was rewarded with part of the proceeds. The buying of
indulgences for ready cash meant a loss of the sense
of sin among the people, and this was further enhanced by the added meaning given to indulgences
during the later Middle Ages.

Now indulgences came to mean the relaxing of
punishment not just by the Church, but by God Him-

self, for the pope, as custodian of that surplus of good
deeds which had been accumulated by the saints through
the ages, was able to grant a remission of divine punishment. Pope Boniface VIII took a further step and
claimed the power to remit the punishment for the
transgression as well as to absolve all guilt incurred in
sinning. Thus by buying an indulgence men had a
right to expect God's mercy. This traffic in indulgences
was bound to offend the pious as a singular abuse of
spiritual power for financial gain. Yet indulgences had
a still more general significance. Easy remittance of sin
legitimized the dissociation of morals and faith, leaving
the door open to that amorality in public and private
life which characterized the period of the Renaissance.

The Indulgence of 1514–1517, which was to arouse
Luther to action, presents a typical story. Albert of
Hohenzollern, already two times a bishop, was ap-
pointed to the important archbishopric of Mainz. Because of this singular instance of "pluralism," he paid
not only the 14,000 ducats usual for an archbishopric,
but also an extra assessment of 10,000 ducats. In order
to help Albert raise the extra money, the papacy sug-
gested the sale of an indulgence, of which Albert was
to receive half of the proceeds and the papacy the other
half, for the building of St. Peter's Cathedral. In spite
of the selling skill of Johann Tetzel, the indulgence was
only a moderate financial success. It proved a political
mistake from the beginning. The elector of Saxony,
rival of the Hohenzollern in the empire, refused to let
it be sold in his dominions, and Martin Luther therefore could not observe Tetzel first-hand.

As far as the papacy was concerned, such financial
policies added to its unpopularity without the cor-
responding advantage of full coffers, for much of the
money remained in the pockets of local rulers, of em-
bezzling functionaries, and of covetous middle men.
The serious consequences which these exactions could
have upon the status of the papacy were illustrated by

the "Gravamina of the German Nation" (1456). This "complaint" was directed against the fiscal policies of Rome, but it proceeded to link financial reform with a more general reform of the clergy, and appealed to the programs proposed at the councils of Constance and Basel. Thus the need for reform kept alive the idea that Christianity by common action could demand changes which the papal monarchy had refused, and was refusing, to carry out.

Next to finance, the need for reform was most urgent in the discipline and customs of the clergy. Here also, the papacy, immersed in the splendor of the Renaissance, could hardly provide leadership. The higher clergy was dominated by secular rulers and served as a means for political advancement or as employment for the younger sons of noble families. The lower clergy suffered from a lack of theological training; in 1535 the archbishop of York was not able to find a dozen clergymen in his diocese who were able to preach a sermon. Similarly, the monasteries and convents gave cause for grave concern. In many of them, communal life had practically ceased, and mundane pleasures dominated those of the spirit. One must beware of generalizations; there were ecclesiastical and religious orders like the Carthusians and the Hieronymites, who maintained a high tradition of spiritual perfection. Yet even before Luther took the leadership into his own hands, these abuses proved real enough to produce not only a demand for reform, but also lay and ecclesiastical movements which tried to accomplish this end. These movements were concerned with revitalizing interest in man's faith and his salvation, concerns which had previously been the main purpose of the Church, and which seemed smothered by the worldly interests of the ecclesiastical hierarchy. If profound piety was not the rule within the organization of the Church, it was still alive among the common people.

Popular Piety. There is abundant evidence of the piety
of the common man at the eve of the Reformation.
Pilgrims crowded the sanctuaries, books of devotion
found a wide audience, and popular preachers could
be assured of full churches. It was a religious ferment
which stressed the emotions rather than the balance
between faith and reason which had been the medieval
ideal. Typical of this piety was the preoccupation with
death; Christ's sufferings on the Cross held a greater
inspiration for the men of the early sixteenth century
than many of his teachings. The theme of the handbooks of devotion was how to escape the eternal tor-
ments of hell. Manuals on the "Art of Dying" depicted
the fate in store for that human who, abandoning the
hope in God's mercy, gave in to the tempting devils
which surrounded him on every side. Dread of the final
judgment, when all men are called up from their graves
to stand before God's judgment seat, added to the
clouds of foreboding under which men lived and died.
Albrecht Dürer, the greatest artist of the age, showed
the horsemen of the Apocalypse, exuberant and joyful,
riding roughshod over the human race. It is significant
that Dürer became one of Luther's most loyal followers
and claimed that Luther's solution to the problem of
spiritual uncertainty had saved him from the abyss of
despair into which he had fallen. Not only Dürer but
other artists like Holbein devoted themselves to de-
picting scenes of death. Holbein's most famous wood-
cut represents a theme common to many artists of
the time, the "Dance of Death," in which king, cardinal,
and commoner dance with death at their backs—skele-
tons made equal by the man with the scythe. It was
to assure himself against eternal death that man made
pilgrimages, bought indulgences, and multiplied masses
for his soul. Driven by this fear, outward signs of
eventual salvation seemed of greatest importance, and
"works" threatened to drive out "faith."

Death and foreboding were not the sole ingredients
of this religious ferment. There was a feeling that a

new era was approaching. Hans Sachs, the poet, assured his countrymen that a new day was at hand. A nebulous feeling of a coming change in the order of things accompanied the constant fear of damnation. Apocalyptical visions became common—the roots of an unbridled religious enthusiasm which was to haunt the reformers. In most spiritual crises, man's troubled soul had found an outlet in mysticism—the idea that man could get into direct touch with God for at least a few moments by exerting his will and ridding his mind of any worldly interests.

This mysticism had a long history behind it. Works of such mystics as St. Bernhard or Bonaventura had served to calm the souls of men in times of stress. In the German Rhineland this movement had found especially fertile soil. Here Meister Eckhardt had, in the fourteenth century, preached a mystic creed until he was expelled from the Church for claiming to be a "fleshy God." Here also his disciples, Suso and Tauler, had given instructions as to how the mystical contact with God might be accomplished. Finally, a compendium of this mystical thought appeared, *The German Theology,* supposedly written by Tauler (1350). Man cannot come to God through learning and study, but only through obedience, through yielding himself to God and abandoning any earthly desires. What does it matter if the Christian is a martyr in this world? Indeed, such martyrdom may help him rid his flesh of unruly affections. This was an attractive creed for times of chaos and change, and of so wide an appeal that Martin Luther was to edit the *Theologia Deutsch* (1516) and to toy with mysticism as a solution to the troubles of his soul.

The causes for these deviations of religious expression in northern Europe are difficult to analyze. Undoubtedly, general social unrest played a part. Undoubtedly, also, the great plagues which had ravaged Europe ever since 1348 were of influence. Moreover, Europe was a beleaguered fortress. The infidel Turk was moving into the heart of Christendom with appalling swiftness. By 1525 he stood before the gates of Vienna. One other factor must be taken into consideration. The popular preaching of the mendicant friars encouraged emotional religion by its appeal to man's sensibilities.

Under the impact of this ferment of popular piety, laymen and clerics attempted to reform themselves. The Oratory of Divine Love in Italy (circa 1517) and the Observant Franciscans in England (1482) were attempts at such reform, but the most significant of these organizations was the Brethren of the Common Life. Starting in the Netherlands, their influence was soon felt in the entire North. The central purpose of this lay brotherhood was the teaching of laymen in the vernacular language (as opposed to the Church's Latin). The essence of their curriculum was an understanding of the classics and of the Bible. Influenced by mysticism, they stressed piety and faith, tempered in their case by learning, as the road to salvation. Out of their schools emerged men like Desiderius Erasmus, and, above all else, Thomas à Kempis, whose *Imitation of Christ* represents one of the greatest handbooks of pious devotion. Besides the Brethren, there were other ecclesiastical orders of strict devotion. Among many Augustinians, in particular, the ideals of faith and salvation had not vanished among worldly concerns or through overemphasis on "works." It was the Augustinians among whom Luther, as a member of the order, had his spiritual awakening; and it was the vicar of Luther's house in Wittenberg, von Staupitz, who became his spiritual guide. His central idea was simplicity of faith, as revealed in the love of God.

This popular piety provided the basis for the popular support of the Reformation. Here the conciliar tradition remained alive, and the quest for the reform of a Church which seemed to have lost touch with popular aspirations was ever present. Long before the masterly satires of Erasmus, popular literature showed itself anticlerical. Sebastian Brant's *Ship of Fools* (1494) compared the clergy to monkeys and castigated those who called themselves shepherds of men's souls but were not fit to be shepherds for the beasts of nature. A contemporary poem in North German dialect made a still more telling point in accusing the clergy of caring for nothing but money, for when the blind lead the blind, both must be parted from God. Thus the blindness of the clergy endangered every man's soul. Here it did little good to point to the papal court as the center of Humanist learning, or to say that the Indulgence of 1517 was to be used to build for Christendom a cathedral worthy of the successors of Saint Peter. The papacy had lost touch with Christian piety in the North; that was to be the central fact of the Reformation. Not the splendor of Raphael or Michelangelo, but the sober and austere woodcuts of Dürer or Holbein were to express the feeling of a Church reformed.

Christian Humanism. The intellectual classes did not stand aside from this ferment of popular piety. The Humanism of Renaissance Italy had put the classics in the center of intellectual life and had, with their aid, recaptured the primacy of individual man. It is true that there were many Italian Humanists who, under the influence of Aristotle or Plato, concerned themselves with the immortality of man's soul, but their concern was not specifically Christian. Three men were instrumental in giving Italian Humanism a Christian and reformist direction, and all three were educated against a background of Northern piety. John Colet in England, Lefèvre in France, and the cosmopolitan Erasmus popularized the application of Humanist learning to specifically Christian problems. They thought it no longer sufficient to cultivate the classics as an art or to go to Plato or Aristotle for spiritual guidance. Instead they dealt with the Word of God itself. The knowledge of the classics was to be used

to purify Biblical texts and to attempt, with the aid of better translations, the interpretation of the Scriptures. Christian Humanism thus found its way back to the Word, and to an emphasis on faith. Erasmus was never tired of lampooning those of his fellow men who made much of outward observances but whose true faith proved a sham. Inevitably these barbs were turned against the unreformed Church, and in books like his *Praise of Folly* (1511) corrupt monks and priests were ruthlessly castigated. But satire was not the only weapon of these intellectuals. Erasmus translated the New Testament from the Greek, and Lefèvre wrote his *Commentary on Saint Paul* (1512), which stressed the sufficiency of the Scriptures for salvation and which, while not rejecting good works, made them consequences of faith rather than prerequisites for it.

Like the Brethren of the Common Life, these Christian Humanists believed strongly in the value of education. Man was essentially good, and through education would be able to choose the right path toward the knowledge of God. John Colet, in London, reformed St. Paul's School, setting up a Humanist curriculum which differed from that of the Brethren by a still greater emphasis upon learning, in order to fit the student for making the right choice. For these learned men believed in the freedom of man's will for good or evil. They were individualists who put man in the center of religious striving.

But freedom of the will had to lead to an informed choice, and this could only be made by those who had acquired knowledge. The learned man, therefore, appears higher in the Humanist hierarchy, and approaches God more closely, than the humble man, the poor in spirit. Erasmus and his fellow Humanists emphasized an aristocracy which was based on intellectual excellence rather than on inherited privilege alone. Influenced by Platonism, they envisaged a society ruled by a learned and therefore enlightened aristocracy and Humanists concentrated on transforming the nobility

of their time into this image. This had some lasting
effect for it coincided with the demands of governments
for "learned men": nobles increasingly sent their chil-
dren to schools and universities. Humanist thought was
aristocratic and here it differed from Luther's concern
which, though placing some emphasis on princes and
rulers, was yet much closer in feeling and texture to
the piety of the common people. Moreover, for Luther
the freedom of man's will, his individualism, was tempered by the power of God and by faith freely received.

The papacy did not condemn these Humanists; indeed Pope Leo X (1513–1521) accepted with gratitude
Erasmus' dedication of his New Testament translation.
Surrounded by Italian Humanists, the Medici pope admired the learning of Erasmus and of his fellow
scholars without paying much heed to their advocacy
of church reform. Nevertheless, there were theologians
in the North who realized better than the papacy the
threat of Christian Humanism to church organization
and who seized the first clear opportunity to force
the issue. The Dominicans of Cologne were in the
forefront of the battle for orthodoxy, and their chance
came when a man named Johannes Pfefferkorn persuaded Emperor Maximilian to support him in a campaign to destroy Hebrew books as tools designed to
lead astray faithful Christians and converted Jews.
The outcry of the Humanists was prompt. The leading Hebraist of the time, Johann Reuchlin, protested
in the name of learning as well as of faith. The universities of Heidelberg and Erfurt, centers of Humanist
learning, joined in the protest. The reply of the
Dominicans was equally prompt; they began an action
for heresy against Reuchlin, while the emperor joined
in the support of the orthodox (1513). Germany was
rent into two camps, with Erasmus leading the Humanists who came to Reuchlin's defense. The defenders
of Humanism resorted to their favorite weapon; in
The Letters of the Obscure Men, an "exposure" of
the Dominican way of life, they presented one of the

most telling satires which literature has to offer. But the suit against Reuchlin went on, and only the death of the aged scholar put him beyond the reach of the Dominicans of Cologne.

The significance of the Reuchlin episode lies in the attempt of religious orthodoxy to stifle that longing for reform which was reflected not only in Christian Humanism but also in the whole spirit of popular piety. Religion had detached itself ever further from the power and influence of church organization. Most of the Christian Humanists, Erasmus among them, never broke with the papacy. The reason for this was a love of peace as conducive to learning, making Erasmus one of the first thoroughgoing pacifists. But there was an additional factor involved. Humanism was a movement of intellectuals, and the "simple faith" of the Wittenberg monk seemed to deny that freedom of the will which was of cardinal importance to these learned men. Yet, to two Humanists, the Reuchlin battle demonstrated that the Church as it existed could no longer be satisfactory as their intellectual home.

Philip Melanchthon and Ulrich von Hutten were men of a very different stamp. Melanchthon, cautious and moderate, was Reuchlin's grand-nephew, a scholar and theologian well fitted to become the diplomatic adviser to Luther in his relations with other reformers. Ulrich von Hutten was an impoverished knight motivated by a deep love for his native Germany and dedicated to protect it against further papal exploitation. Luther needed both the moderation of Melanchthon and the nationalistic ardor of Hutten. But it was Melanchthon who remained at his side to the last, and Hutten who died, repudiated and forgotten, on a lonely island in a Swiss lake. If, for all his learning, Luther failed to join the ranks of the Humanists, yet he shared their love of peace and hatred of rebellion. In spite of this, he was constantly forced to restrain Melanchthon's penchant for compromise, lest matters essential for salvation be prejudiced. Melanchthon feared nothing so much as the charge of sedition, while Luther was willing to risk sedition for the sake of certainty of salvation. Thus the religious ferment of the times had a greater influence upon him than the calm learning of the intellectuals, and in the end he castigated Erasmus as representing *verba sine re*, "words without deeds," as meaningless to Luther as the faith of the clergy in *The Praise of Folly* had been to Erasmus. Perhaps the greatest difference between Luther and these intellectuals was that while they taught reform, Luther lived it. For him the cause was not a matter of the intellect, but of the soul, and of the soul only.

Justification by Faith. Popular piety flourished amidst the forests of the remote German region of Thuringia. For the peasants and craftsmen of that country God was ever present and salvation a constant concern. Martin Luther was the son of Thuringian peasants who had attained modest middle class wealth. Reared against a background of popular piety, young Martin was determined to become a monk and to devote his life to the service of God. While his devotion to the inward life was aided by his schooling by some Brethren of the Common Life, he first came into close contact with orthodox theology at the University of Erfurt, not as yet touched by Humanist learning. The theology taught at Erfurt was the theology of the Englishman William of Occam, which had found acceptance by the Church. Occam stressed the absolutism of God, who could save or condemn by His will alone. Yet Occam admitted the *possibility* that man, through his own force of will, could prepare the ground for salvation. What this theology meant to a sensitive and pious soul like Luther's was a growing uncertainty, a feeling of being buffeted between God's absolutism and man's possibility of preparing for salvation through his own power. Where, in this theology, was certainty to be found? Luther's struggle of the spirit and his frequent depressions were centered around the problem of how man can be certain of that salvation for which his soul searches.

These spiritual struggles did not end when Luther fulfilled his life's goal by entering the Augustinian priory at Erfurt (1505). They were further enhanced by his glimpse of life at the papal court during his one visit to Rome (1510). Pomp and splendor proved no solution for a hungry soul in the quest of salvation. Before he had journeyed to Rome, Luther had been transferred to the Augustinian priory at Wittenberg (1508); and here, where he was to make his home for the rest of his life, he faced the spiritual crisis which was to transform his own life and the lives of his fellow men.

It was von Staupitz, the vicar of the priory, who first tried to lighten the load which seemed to rest on the troubled spirit of this young monk. Staupitz's mild mysticism attracted Luther. He thought that this heightening of popular piety by the attempt to fuse one's soul with God might solve the quest for certainty. Yet Luther never became a disciple of the mystics; he was unable to quiet his soul by immersing it in the Creator. To him the mystical experience was a momentary one, and did not lead to permanent peace of the soul. Staupitz decided to try another medicine. He gave Luther a teaching position at the University. His subject matter was the Bible. He commenced by teaching the Psalms and by 1515 he was teaching the Epistles of St. Paul. It was while performing his daily task of teaching that Luther resolved the great conflict between the mercy and the wrath of God, and it was St. Paul who was his inspiration, just as the Apostle had inspired Lefèvre to a belief in the primacy of faith.

The connection between St. Paul and the reform movement is not difficult to trace. The Apostle had criticized the early Christian Church, just as these men were criticizing the Church of their day, and for much the same reasons. For St. Paul, too, there had been the danger of substituting the Church for the Scriptures and the church hierarchy for God's faith. If for St. Paul many members of the Church were confining the grace of God within the limitations of the Jewish Torah, so for Luther that grace was imprisoned within the walls of theological orthodoxy. In this way, the Epistles of St. Paul played a very real part in the Reformation, and seemed especially relevant to the problems of the late medieval Church as Martin Luther saw them.

"Night and day I pondered until I saw the connection between the justice of God and the statement, 'The righteous shall live by his faith.' Then I grasped that the justice of God is that righteousness by which through grace and sheer mercy God justifies us through faith. Thereupon I felt myself to be reborn and to have gone through open doors into Paradise." Thus Martin Luther arrived at salvation through faith alone; his quest for spiritual certainty had been solved. Faith is not an achievement; it is a gift which comes to man through the hearing and the study of the Word. Luther had studied the Bible for his lectures, and had come to see the solution to his spiritual problems. Faith justifies man before God, and it is part of that faith to trust God, to believe that he is, through Christ, constantly striving to save mankind. This insight was to be the motivating force of Luther's life and work. All else was but a commentary upon it.

It was after he had reached this central conclusion that Luther encountered the Indulgence of 1517. Here was an action directly opposed to his new-found certainty and conviction, a substitution of works for faith. Already, prior to 1517, Luther had begun to preach against the growing number of indulgences which were being sold throughout Germany. But the numbers in which the citizens of Wittenberg went to acquire Tetzel's indulgences, and then demanded that on their

presentation they be absolved from sin, brought matters
to a head. Luther was shocked by the fact that the
archbishop of Mainz could be a party to such practices,
and was naïvely sure that the pope would disapprove.
As he wrote to the archbishop, his theses were meant
not to create strife, but to prevent it. He did not broad-
cast his views throughout the land, but posted them on
the bulletin board of the university at the castle church.
These ninety-five theses were a call to theological disputation as well as an appeal to the conscience of
the archbishop. The first of these theses shows how
the whole practice of indulgences ran counter to
Luther's conviction of salvation by faith: "If Christ,
our Lord and Master says, 'Do penance,' he wants the
entire life of the pious to be one penance." Penance
was the humility of faith, and had nothing to do with
atonement through works or through the payment of
money. October 31, 1517, was meant by Luther to mark
the starting point in rectifying an obvious abuse which
did damage to the Church. Instead, this date marks
the beginning of his break with Rome.

"He has touched the crown of the pope and the
stomachs of the monks." Erasmus' evaluation of the importance of Luther's action proved correct. The financial interests of the papacy were attacked, and the
echo which Luther's action aroused among the people
imperiled the whole success of the Indulgence. Once
again, as in the Reuchlin affair, the Dominicans pressed
for action against Luther. But now they overplayed
their hand, for it was the disputations, in which Luther
had to defend his faith against orthodox theologians,
that gained him nation-wide attention. Already after
his first public defense at Augsburg (1518) before the
kindly papal legate Cajetan, it was said that Luther
was the most famous man in Germany. The most
crucial of these disputations took place at Leipzig
(1519) with the able and violently orthodox Johannes
Eck. Through his cogent argumentation as Luther's
adversary, Eck pushed Luther into questioning the

John Hus Burned at the Stake. (*Three Lions*)

divine appointment of the papacy and, worse, into admitting a sympathy with some of the ideas of both Wycliffe and Hus. The customary public disputation of theological points had led Luther into a heretical position, for he was forced to argue out the consequences of his central belief in "justification by faith," and to approach ever nearer the idea of the primacy of all believers over any church organization. This was the core of that religious individualism to which Lutheranism inevitably led. Why should the Church have a pope if Christ was her head? Every believer was a priest insofar as he had found faith and had been justified by God through his faith. At Leipzig these consequences of his belief were as yet to be sought underneath Luther's guarded language, though Eck correctly divined them. But one year later, the papacy itself acted. Luther was condemned as a heretic in the bull *Exsurge* (1520). He had to retract or stand in danger of becoming a revolutionary. Owing to the certainty of his convictions, Luther had no choice. Before the assembled students of the University of Wittenberg, the professor of Bible committed to the flames the bull which placed him outside the Church.

The University of Wittenberg was in sympathy with the gesture of its professor, and from this University a whole series of disciples were to go out among their fellow men to educate them in the Lutheran faith. Luther had by now gained attention far beyond the confines of the Saxon town. He had won the ear of the nation, and he now used this popular appeal to further his cause through the printed word. It was fortunate for Luther that the printing press had been developed by the time of the Reformation (1450), and he made full use of this new invention. All the reformers were to rely heavily on the printed word in spreading their message, drawing ever wider circles into the controversies of the age. In a real sense this was the first use of books as propaganda weapons, and here, too, Luther pioneered. His scurrilous language, which has shocked subsequent ages, was meant to bring home the truth of the gospel to people untouched by intellectual refinements—people for whom the elegant satires of the Christian Humanists were too subtle and not forceful enough to drive home the point. The year 1521 saw Luther's ideas spelled out for all the world to read.

The Tracts of 1520–1521. The three great tracts of 1520–1521 clarify Luther's principal religious ideas. In the *Babylonish Captivity of the Church,* he used the force of his language to castigate the abuses of the Church, while going beyond the abuses themselves by advocating actual change in liturgy. Because the *Babylonish Captivity* abolished several central rites of the Church, it was thought by contemporaries to be his most radical tract and confirmed his irrevocable breach with the papacy. His keynote was the perversion of the sacraments by the Church, and he reduced them to two in number; the Lord's Supper and Baptism alone remained, for only these two seemed to Luther to have been directly instituted by Christ. His belief in the supremacy of faith dictated the abolition of priestly absolution from sin as a vital part of penance, because man cannot anticipate the decision of God. The denying of ordination for priests dealt a severe blow to the clergy as a special caste, and put them on an equal footing with the rest of the believers. To Luther all Christians were priests. Abolition of Ordination as a sacrament had another consequence. It reduced the Catholic Mass to a celebration of communion or the Lord's Supper. No longer was the priest alone endowed with the power to perform the miracle of the bread and wine. No longer, therefore, was the Church the sole custodian of the body of Christ. Instead, the religious service became the concern of the whole congregation of the faithful, a communal action in which the entire priesthood of believers participated.

The symbol for this full participation in the religious

service was the hymn. The Gregorian chants of the
Church had been so technical that they were sung by
special choirs or by priests. Luther adapted the German
folk song to religious poetry and thus made it possible
for all the faithful to participate fully in every part
of the service. He composed at least thirty-seven of
these hymns, and in 1524 published the first evangelical
hymnbook. Thus the transformation of the liturgy as
put forward in the *Babylonish Captivity* eventually
meant the beginning of the great age of Protestant
church music, which found its climax over a hundred
years later in the chorals of Johann Sebastian Bach
(1685-1750).

In adapting German folk music for his hymns,
Luther showed again his close affinity with the spirit
of his own people. That same spirit is evidenced in his
*Appeal to the Christian Nobility of the German Na-
tion*. It was to the Germans that he addressed himself,
and here the influence of Ulrich von Hutten is apparent—Hutten, who had urged Luther to break with
Rome, not so much for theological reasons, but because he could be of use as a figure symbolizing national resentment against papal exploitation. For
Luther, however, the fact that he addressed himself
to Germany was always incidental to his religious program. If the *Babylonish Captivity* dealt with liturgy,
the *Appeal* was directed toward the problem of church
organization.

Luther advised the German ruling classes that by
God's command it was the duty of the magistrates to
punish evildoers, and called upon them to repulse the
pretensions of the Roman Church. But Luther went
beyond this; the magistrates were called upon to reform
the Church, to strip it of worldly power and wealth
which disguised and smothered true faith. Thus he
began to endow the rulers with ecclesiastical functions,
for were they not baptized and Christians like any-
body else? If the worldly power of the clergy had to
vanish in the name of a reinvigorated faith, then some-

one else had to assure that there was "order" in the affairs of the Church, and that must be the magistrate who was set by God over men, and who shared in the priesthood of all believers. It was not to curry favor with the princes that Luther gave them authority over church organization, but as a natural consequence of the equality of all believers.

To Luther, the external order of the Church was of secondary importance. For this reason, in his *German Mass* (1525), he disclaimed any intention of making his order of service a law for his church. Salvation by faith was, after all, an individual matter. For all that, Luther did not intend unbridled individualism. St. Paul teaches us that we must see to it that we have the same ideals; are we not all born in the same way? Baptized in the same way? Do we not have the same sacraments? God has not given special dispensation to anyone. In this way, princes or city councils could regulate the Church, asserting that they were seeing to it that "due order" was observed.

Luther tried to follow a moderate course, but the outcome of his ideas on church organization was the alliance between altar and throne which was to make Lutheranism a state church, thus strengthening the hand of the government against dissent. Ultimately, such a theory was bound to provide support for that absolutism whose emergence to prominence dominates the political thought of the sixteenth and seventeenth centuries. As the maintenance of Christian life and morality was transferred from the hand of a discredited Church to the supervision of the State, men were to find an outlet for their credulity in admiration for the God-fearing prince. And that prince, free from the interference of a universal Church, could use his God to justify arbitrary government over his people. If this absolutism was to be facilitated as a consequence of Luther's church organization, what, then, did he mean by Christian liberty? This is the theme of his third great tract, *Concerning the Liberty of a Christian Man*.

The liberty with which Luther dealt was not outward political or social freedom, but the inward liberty which comes from a faith found. The liberty of justification before God has good works as a natural consequence, but good works themselves have nothing to do with this liberty. "Good works do not make a man good, but a good man does good works." God has given great riches to the world and the man worthy of them through faith will do all to please God. He will give himself to his neighbor, as Christ gave Himself to mankind. However, the Christian must not reject such happy hours as God confers upon him, and the good doctor himself spent many happy hours over his glass of beer, or over a game of cards. It is important to remember, however, that Christians were not authorized to break through the bonds of class and social distinctions, or even to reach for political power. It was not that Luther was indifferent to the downtrodden, but to him, for whom inner freedom and certainty were the only concerns, worldly rebellion was a sign of insufficient attention to the real business of life, which lay in the attainment of faith and not in the gathering of riches.

With the year 1521, Luther's views were fully revealed and elaborated upon. Typically enough, he still dedicated *The Liberty of a Christian Man* to Pope Leo X, in the faint hope of a reconciliation. But even if the idea of Christian liberty might prove acceptable, Luther had burned his bridges behind him in the other tracts. He now faced the world not as a reformer, but as a heretic. Not only the Church was taking notice of the Wittenberg professor, but the worldly authorities had to take a stand also.

The Diet of Worms. The chief worldly authority in Germany was the emperor, and Luther's break with the Church came at a time when a new emperor had just been elected (1519). The great problem which faced the emperors in their German dominions was the keeping of order amidst the constant weakening of central government. Since the emperor was not a hereditary monarch, but elected by certain of the chief princes, he was forced to make extensive concessions in order to obtain his office. Emperor Maximilian (1493–1519) had tried to order the affairs of the empire, but the resistance of the princes had proved too great an obstacle. In reality Germany was a network of princely states, each prince consolidating his position within his dominion and competing for power with neighboring German states. Some of these states were ecclesiastical principalities, while others were free cities, towns like Nürnberg or Strassburg which were "free" in the sense that they were under sole imperial authority, and therefore behaved like other princely states. If the princes were the most powerful and decisive element in the empire, there were two others also worthy of notice.

The formerly powerful estate of knights was being harried from all sides. Gunpowder and mercenary troops robbed them of useful employment, and the merchant classes pressed them economically. Thus they became robber barons, to whom adventure meant livelihood. It was from this class that Ulrich von Hutten came, and his nationalism was shared by his fellow knights, for they saw in "foreign" Rome the scapegoat upon which they could blame their troubles. Thus they were inclined to embrace reform as protection for Germany against the papal exploitation from which all evil flowed. The peasants, as the lowest estate in the empire, did not all suffer equally. In the West the peasants had attained a certain prosperity, while in the East—where the soil was more barren—great estates were the only economically feasible way of farming, and the peasants lived in a state of serfdom. The peasants of the West were responsible for the element of unrest because they found their position endangered by the encroachments of the local nobility, aided by the

princes. Legal changes unfavorable to their independence also excited their animosity. The agrarian problem in the sixteenth century was prevalent throughout
Europe. It meant the oppression of individual peasants through the consolidation of large estates and the
liquidation of their "customary" but unwritten privileges. Here were classes of the population for whom
Luther's teaching could not only give spiritual certainty,
but could also, through the individualism of the
Protestant faith, point toward goals of social and
economic emancipation.

Into this situation stepped the new emperor in 1520,
nearly two years after his election—years which had
meant further chaos in the empire and which had
increased popular longing for peace and quiet. Charles
of Hapsburg, already ruler of Spain and the Netherlands, came to his new dominion amidst a chorus of
popular acclaim in which Luther joined. Charles V
(1519–1556) was a man of limited intellect, passionately
devoted to duty; as the chief duty of a ruler was to
keep order, where was a firm hand more necessary than
in Germany? Charles considered the preservation of
religious orthodoxy the principal part of preserving
order. The Diet of Worms (1521) was to strengthen
Charles in this conviction, for though, in the general
atmosphere of good will toward the new emperor,
progress was made in strengthening central authority,
the Lutheran issue was to nullify any attempt at order
within the empire, making Charles's rule one of con-
tinual trouble and growing unpopularity.

The very fact that Luther was summoned to the diet
demonstrated to what extent the issues raised by the
excommunicated monk had become national issues. It
was the diet which pressed the emperor to give Luther
a hearing before the nation, and it was the estates which
refused to sanction the burning of Luther's books, so
that the emperor had to accomplish this by a personal
decree. Luther had truly become a national figure, and,

as such, he was compared in the German mind with
the other great national figure, Charles V. But it was
Charles who was the newcomer, for in the years between Maximilian's death and Charles's entry into Germany, Martin Luther had emerged as the symbol of
a possible solution to the national and spiritual chaos
within the empire. Not only had he found supporters
among the knights and the peasants but—politically
more important—he had found friends among the
princes as well. When Luther, at Worms, refused to
retract his opinions, and defied worldly might as he had
earlier defied the Church, he was again thinking in
theological terms; but whether he liked it or not, his
fate was now bound up with the strainings and strivings
within the empire, which were by no means solely
spiritual in character. The ban of the empire (1521),
which Charles hurled against him, proved no more
effective than the ban of the Church.

For Martin Luther, the ban meant a time in retire-
ment at Wartburg Castle (1521-1522), which was not
spent in idleness but in fashioning a German translation of the Bible. For although he was under the ban
of empire, he enjoyed the effective protection of
Frederick the Wise, elector of Saxony. Frederick in his
own way was as pious as the emperor and by no means
a rebel against the Church. Indeed, he had been the
pope's candidate for the office of emperor, but because
of both personal modesty and calculations of political
power, he had refused to accept the candidacy. His
support of Luther was at first reluctant, and due to
the fact that Luther was a professor at his cherished
University of Wittenberg. Only gradually did Frederick
become one of the leaders against Charles's attempt to
get order into the empire and to curtail the political
power of the princes. However, in the process of this
resistance to a central authority supporting religious
orthodoxy, Frederick became convinced also of the
validity of Luther's faith.

The Radicals. Meanwhile, Luther was no longer alone in the field. He had attracted fellow travelers who threatened to jeopardize his cause even before it was properly established. The new evangelical faith threatened to become a slogan for all sorts of liberties, from the liberty of a Christian man to the liberty of the robber baron. For with the uprooting of church organization, all was threatened by social and political chaos.

The knights thought that their day had come at last, for their oppressors, the cities and the princes, were locked in a bitter quarrel at the Diet of Worms. The princes were in debt to the cities, and the cities could not make further concessions without imperiling their "free" status. The leader of the knight class, Franz von Sickingen, had long been a close friend of Hutten, and as an early supporter of Martin Luther he had sheltered and protected the doctor on his journeys. He thought that here was his opportunity to strike a blow for the reform of church and empire. Sickingen sought to accomplish his aims and to settle a private feud by a piratical attack on the archbishopric of Trier, hoping to rally both Lutheran support and the cities in the attack on this ecclesiastical principality (1522). He had underestimated the solidarity of the princes. Not only was Trier saved, but the cities failed to come to his support, Sickingen's castles were demolished, and he was killed. Luther stood aside from this action by his friends; had he put his trust in the knights, he would have gone down with them. Hutten had to flee Germany, repudiated by Luther, whose fortunes he had hitherto shared.

Meanwhile, Luther was busy closer to home, where he seemed to have fathered civil disturbances instead of justification by faith. His own Wittenberg saw the first violent popular eruption which was an attempt to bring about reform overnight. During Luther's absence, Carlstadt had assumed Protestant leadership in the town. The Wittenberg town council, under his guidance, issued the first city ordinance of the Reformation (1522). The Catholic Mass was abolished, as were all images in the churches. Wittenberg, in spite of warnings from Frederick, proceeded to vent its fury on images and priests. But this was not all. Several men arrived from neighboring Zwickau claiming to have established personal contact with the Lord, and disclaiming the need for scripture. If the Bible was so important, God would have dropped it directly from heaven. These "enthusiasts" created another uproar in the city. Luther had to return from the Wartburg castle to restore order. Although he succeeded in this instance, the floodgates which had opened to mystical ferment were never to close, and were to plague not only him, but all future reformers.

The Anabaptists. Because the efficacy of infant baptism was denied, this religious radicalism went under the name of Anabaptism. Only those who had "received the spirit" could be true Christians and therefore worthy of baptism. This attitude toward baptism was part of a system of thought which was truly revolutionary. True Christians were a clearly defined group of men and women who were the elect and thus sinless. Such perfectionism did lead to the idea that actions normally sinful were not sinful for the elect and this, in turn, led some Anabaptists into moral excesses. The Lutherans and Calvinists emphasized these eccentricities in their efforts to combat Anabaptism and bombarded the movement with a barrage of hostile propaganda. What has been obscured by this propaganda is the really revolutionary content of their doctrine, for the Anabaptists were closely linked to Millenarianism. The Millennium was imminent and those who were the elect must now form a society on truly Christian principles. It is essential here, to realize that Anabaptism was a lower-class movement. It expressed in a more violent form the hope for a better life: in the

Millennium, when Christ returned, all would be equal; there would be neither rich nor poor. For this reason the society of the truly baptized had to be an equalitarian one.

These ideas were not new. Their antecedents can be found in medieval heresies and even in a part of the Hussite movement in Bohemia. Plainly, this admixture of a sect of the elect based on the spirit, denying external signs of election and believing in the advent of the Millennium expressed a real "Christianity of the poor." It received a new impulse through the Reformation, through those sentiments expressed by the reformers exalting "liberty" and praising the humble. Moreover, Anabaptism depended on the "prophet" who would gather the group together and lead them to triumph over the pagans, that is the others who mistakenly called themselves "Christian." Thomas Münzer was such a prophet. For him those "reborn" in the spirit had a mission to build the Kingdom of God on earth in the expectation of the Millennium. This would require a struggle with the unregenerate and their subsequent extermination. For Münzer the poor, free from the temptation of avarice and luxury, were the elect who would inaugurate the new Millennium. With the doctrine that God revealed himself daily to his elect, Münzer could give a dynamism to his religious experimentation. When Münzer asserted that clergymen and theologians were "snakes" who misled the people, when he proclaimed the office of ruler to be a heathen one, he spoke as a prophet of God, vouchsafing new revelations. In order to transform society into a Christian commonwealth a new Daniel must arise and, like Moses, lead the faithful. Münzer cast himself in this role.

Twice he assumed leadership. First, he tried to build the godly society in Mülhausen in Thuringia (1525), and then he led the Thuringian peasants in the peasant wars. In both cases he relied on a hard core of followers known as the "League of the Elect." He

never gave himself time to accomplish much at Mülhausen, leaving almost at once to exhort the revolting
peasants to fight, for they were the elect. "At them,
at them, while the fire is hot! One cannot speak of
God as long as they are reigning over you. God goes
ahead of you so follow, follow!" The failure of the
peasants' revolt was Münzer's undoing, and he was
captured and beheaded in the camp of the princes
(May 1525).

The new Jerusalem did come about, not in Mülhausen or through the peasants, but in the city of
Münster in Westphalia (February 1534 – June 1535).
Here the Anabaptists captured the city council, and
after expelling many of the unbelievers they proceeded
to construct the City of God on earth in the form of
a primitive communistic society. No one, for example,
was allowed to possess money; indeed all goods were
shared and food was served from a common kitchen.
Polygamy was eventually instituted. It solved a very
pressing problem. Those who had fled the city had, in
a good many cases, left their womenfolk behind them,
and men were needed to provide for their subsistence.

Conflict arose at the weakest point in the Anabaptist
structure: the rival claims of prophets, each thinking
himself the new Daniel. John of Leyden won the power
struggle within the city and proclaimed himself king.
A rule of terror followed, accentuated by the continuous siege of the city by neighboring princes. John
of Leyden, the king and prophet, himself executed his
enemies with a sword on the market place. Yet Münster
withstood its siege longer and more successfully than
did almost any other city in that age. There was a
millennial spirit within the walls, a sense that a new
and truly Christian society would prevail. It did not.
John of Leyden was put to the sword as were many
of the Anabaptists who had defended the city.

After the Münster experience Anabaptists turned
quietist and pacific. Instead of trying to change society,
they formed enclaves of righteousness withdrawn from

a pagan world. The impetus for this kind of Anabaptism already existed. Its origins lay in Switzerland and its founder was Conrad Grebel (1495?–1526) of Zurich. There, strict allegiance to the Bible triumphed over millenarian prophecy. The stress upon a true community of believers remained, indeed it received increasing emphasis. Individualism was a sin against God; a perfect community required economic as well as spiritual union with one's fellow believers. Such a community lived a life of its own, rejecting any participation in the pagan state and stressing nonviolence. At first called "Swiss Brethren," these men came to typify the Anabaptism of the sixteenth century, though they were never united into a coherent organization.

Yet the image of the society which had been attempted at Münster never died. The disenfranchised continued to grasp at the revolutionary dynamic of this thought, and it comes to the surface whenever the existing order is successfully challenged. Thus a similar Anabaptism is found among the Puritan radicals during the English revolution just as it can be found once more in the industrially backward regions of Europe in the nineteenth century. Clearly, Luther had to cope with an outbreak of radicalism which was not peculiar to the Reformation. Revolutionary millenarianism had its roots in the medieval past and it would still possess a dynamic force long after Luther was dead. The relatively short span of fifteen years, from the prophets of Zwickau (1520) to the Münster fiasco (1535), during which the movement plagued the reformers was only a brief episode in what would be a long and stormy career. For the poor this was the true revolution and they sought to make it a reality whenever they could, especially because the Reformation proved a bitter disappointment to them.

The Peasant Wars. The experiment at Münster was less of a menace for Martin Luther than the earlier peasant wars. Here the "true revolution" was not confined to a city but embraced, however chaotically, by a whole class of the population. Both economic and many political grievances drove the German peasants in the west of the empire to strive for a radical change in their situation. For these were the peasants who were rather prosperous; those who were virtual serfs in the eastern part of the empire did not join the uprising. The Western peasant felt that his status in society was slipping and his economic patrimony was endangered. The application of Roman law put into question that land which they had held by immemorial custom and for which they could show no record of ownership. A newly strengthened commercial economy further endangered their situation. Moreover the lords, themselves pressed for money, attempted to convert the traditional dues into money rents. All these factors meant a disorientation, a sense of being pushed to the wall, which drew the peasants to Luther and his doctrines and then pushed them on to rally to the standard of Thomas Münzer.

The priesthood of all believers could lead to demands for social and political equality—indeed, Carlstadt had already arrived at such an interpretation. Luther's criticism of usury had scriptural justification, but it could become a rallying point against exploitation. Luther's position in the revolt is obscured, for he talked two languages in an attempt to calm the unrest. To the princes he justified many of the demands of the peasants, while to the peasants he spoke sternly against transforming the liberty of the spirit into the liberty of the flesh. What Luther feared above all was the active implementation of the peasants' demands, for revolt by private subjects against magistrates was contrary to the will of God. Nothing would ensue but murder and bloodshed. Luther was correct. The uprising was put down with as much cruelty as the peasants had shown in plundering castles and estates. Lack of organization was the peasants' undoing. Theirs was not one revolt, but a series of regional uprisings. At the Battle of Frankenhausen (1525) the princes defeated the largest group of the peasants led by Thomas Münzer. The result of the Peasants' Revolt for the Reformation was twofold. It cost Luther the support of many of the common people, whom he had, as they saw it, abandoned in a moment of crisis. The rebellion acted on Luther as a catalytic agent. He now feared chaos as he had formerly feared the devil. This fear made him increasingly intolerant of any form of Protestantism other than his own, and this in turn meant the loss of large regions to rival reforming movements. This intolerance is further clarified by Luther's attitude toward Protestant unity.

Marburg and Augsburg. That the problem of Protestant unity could arise at all testifies to the fact that Luther's example was being followed. Not only Zwingli in the Swiss city of Zurich, but Martin Bucer in Strassburg also had found adherents who, in contrast to the enthusiasts, were firmly established in their localities, and who had become respectable partisans of the Protestant cause. The idea was already current that these Protestant groups should join with Lutheranism and present a common program and a common confederation in order to strengthen their position. Typically enough, the pressure for unity came from political rather than from theological considerations. Philip of Hesse, who had joined the elector of Saxony in the leadership of the Protestant princes, convoked a conference of the chief Protestant theologians in his castle at Marburg (1529). There was need for the formulation of a common policy, for at the approaching Diet of Augsburg, Protestants would once more have to defend their views. The parley failed for theological reasons; Luther had little understanding of politics, and he again voiced his abhorrence of the violence that might arise from any aggressive, or even defensive, Protestant alliance.

The gospel should not be the cause for the shedding

of blood. What he had not condoned for the peasants, he was not going to condone for the princes, that is, that the duly constituted order be overthrown. Luther, under political pressure, was in no mood for compromise on matters of faith. It was the dispute over the nature of the Lord's Supper which prevented agreement among the Protestant leaders. Luther violently opposed the interpretations put forward by the other reformers. He believed that Christ was present in the elements of bread and wine, and that to view the sacrament of Communion in any other way was sacrilege. Melanchthon backed Luther against the views of the others. The lay leaders of Saxony were consulted, and the paramount significance of the religious factor was brought out once again when the Saxon chancellor sided with Luther, choosing a belief he thought right rather than a politically expedient alliance among Protestants.

The Marburg colloquy had serious consequences for the Protestant cause. By means of the Wittenberg Concord (1536), Bucer and Melanchthon managed ultimately to find a formula which permitted agreement among the North German Protestants, but the Swiss and the South German cities, which belonged to the Zwinglian party, were permanently detached from Lutheranism. For the Protestant princes, the situation also had a serious aspect. Allies were lost or deserted, and Protestant disunity was underlined when three separate statements of their views were presented at the Diet of Augsburg (1530). One was the famous Augsburg Confession of the Lutheran party, another the *Confessio Tetrapolitana,* drawn up by Bucer, and a third was presented by the Swiss. Of these, the Augsburg Confession is the most important, for it was to be *the* significant Lutheran confession of faith, formulated by Melanchthon, counseled and strengthened by Luther. It set forth in a systematic way the ideas which had already been expressed in the great tracts of the Reformation. The proud citation on the title page read, "I will speak of Thy testimonies also before kings, and will not be ashamed" (Psalm 119). Ashamed the Protestants were not; the name "Protestant" had already been given to them a year (1529) before this diet.

Luther realized that there was no longer any hope for unanimity of faith within the empire. That this realization proved correct was partly due to the fact that for the next fifteen years the harried Charles V was too busy with Turks and French to intervene effectively in the empire. With the absence of central control, Lutheranism could better take root and develop. In this it was aided by Luther's translation of the Bible. He began publishing parts of the Scriptures in 1522, and twelve years later the whole translation was printed (1534). Not only was the Word thus given to the German people, but their language was enriched and standardized. Once again Luther adapted local dialects as he had adapted folk songs for his hymns. The basic language he used was the court tongue of the electorate of Saxony, and its use in his Biblical translation was eventually to make it the universal German tongue of "High German." The Augsburg Confession and the German Bible marked the definite establishment of Lutheranism. Though the Church had weathered schism and councils, it had failed to cope with the third challenge—the German Reformation.

The Final Crisis. A final crisis had to be surmounted before Lutheranism could enjoy full security, and that came at the moment when Charles, free from other worries, could at last devote himself to the affairs of the empire. Luther did not live to see the war which he would have deplored. He died in the very year (1546) that the struggle between the Protestant princes and the emperor broke out in full force. The Lutheran princes, who had formed a loose alliance among themselves at Schmalkalden (1530), were decisively defeated at the battle of Mühlberg (1547). It was Luther's political ineptitude which helped prepare this defeat, for the personal failure of Philip of Hesse's leadership was due to the advice of both Luther and Bucer regarding his marriage. They had condoned the Hessian's bigamous marriage with a lady of his court. Such a marriage not only weakened the moral authority of the Reformation, but also put Philip in conflict with the criminal laws of the empire. Philip was frightened and, in return for Charles's forgiveness, promised to make no separate alliances with foreign powers. Thus the Lutheran princes were kept from an alliance with France which might have strengthened their cause and led to victory instead of defeat.

Once victorious, Charles overplayed his hand. In the Interim (1548), he undertook to reimpose Catholicism upon the empire, with a few minor concessions to Protestant practices. While attempting to restore the traditional faith, Charles tried to strengthen his own position. He imprisoned the princes of Saxony and Hesse as a gesture of defiance to all other princes who might oppose his will. Moreover, the emperor tried to get his son, Philip II, recognized as his successor in the empire; Philip was a Spaniard, an utter foreigner to Germany.

Charles combined this enforcement of his will on the empire with a conciliatory gesture which sent his "foreign" Spanish troops home and thus deprived himself of solid military backing. The result was a swift reversal of his victory. The princes, now strengthened by a secret alliance with France, stirred up resistance against the emperor. They united against Charles; the maintenance of political power proved more important than religious divergence among themselves. Taken by surprise, Charles fled across the Alps (1552) attended only by a few faithful retainers.

The time was ripe for a settlement. The emperor's defeat had conclusively demonstrated the strength of princely power and of Lutheranism. Within the empire

Charles's defeat also spelled the end of his hopes for Philip's succession to the Hapsburg heritage. It was Charles's brother, Ferdinand, who was destined to become the next emperor (1556). At the diet called again at Augsburg (1555), Ferdinand, acting for Charles, accepted the compromise which was to mean the final establishment of Lutheranism in the empire. The principle underlying the peace reflected the realities of the political situation, *cujus regio, ejus religio*. Every prince was to determine the faith, Lutheran or Catholic, of his principality. Those citizens whose faith was different from that of the ruler were assured free emigration. In the "ecclesiastical reservation" an attempt was made to save the territories of the Roman Catholic Church from Protestantism. Any bishop who became Protestant lost his bishopric with all its territories and income. This peace was supposed to be a provisional settlement, but it lasted for sixty-three years, and Germany became an island of peace amidst the religious wars which broke out in other West European countries. The peace of Augsburg could last because it reflected the true political situation within the empire; failure to crush the new heresy had also meant failure to constitute a strong political authority exercised by the emperor, and Germany was now a region of several hundred principalities and free cities, governed by princes, bishops, and burghers.

The Lutheran Reformation did not, however, lead directly to princely absolutism, as many historians have charged. To be sure, the princes themselves desired to extend the powers they had obtained over the Church to the entire government of their territories. But their estates proved too strong; indeed, control over the Church in many cases benefited the estates as much as it did the rulers themselves. Only the duke of Bavaria managed to established an absolutist form of Government, and he was a Catholic hostile to Protestantism. It took another century for the princes to crush their estates effectively; the seventeenth century, not the sixteenth, was to be the age of absolutism. Lutheranism and the Peace of Augsburg contributed to this development only in an indirect manner.

The final establishment of the Reformation was thus linked with political factors as well as with purely religious considerations. The spread of the Lutheran Reformation outside Germany followed a similar pattern. In Scandinavia, Lutheranism was established by the monarchies. In Sweden, Gustavus Vasa proclaimed the reformed religion in 1527, and by confiscating the goods of the Church accumulated enough revenue to complete his successful revolt against Danish domination. In Denmark, Christian II was spiritually attracted to Luther and fathered the break with Rome at the assembly of Odensee (1527); the diet of Copenhagen approved a Lutheran liturgy in the same year that the Augsburg Confessions were set forth in Germany (1530).

At the other end of Europe, Primus Truber introduced the Lutheran reform into Slovenia (1547). Like Luther, he exerted a profound cultural influence, for his translation of the Bible standardized the Slovenian language just as Luther had fathered a common German tongue. In Bohemia and Hungary, Lutheranism penetrated and scored initial successes; but here, as in France and the Netherlands, Luther's faith was to be replaced by Calvinism. Practically speaking, Lutheranism had lost its dynamic quality by the time of Luther's death. But the force of Calvinism was only beginning to be felt, and it was to the faith of Calvin that much of the future belonged. Yet Luther had provided the inspiration for his Protestant successors, however much his Protestantism differed from theirs.

C H A P T E R . . . 3

A Continued Reformation

Ulrich Zwingli

For over two centuries after Luther's death, the most active and influential form of Protestantism was that of John Calvin. The French reformer made a synthesis of the Protestantisms which had preceded his, borrowing one idea here, another there, and transforming all into a coherent whole. It has become common usage to speak of *the* Reformation, as if there had been only one, or at least two, which had a lasting influence on the course of events. But Luther and Calvin were not the only important reformers; there were at least two others of considerable stature and influence—Ulrich Zwingli of Zurich and Martin Bucer of Strassburg.

Ulrich Zwingli had been awakened to active interest in reform through the "monkish quarrel" in Germany. Yet Zwingli's background was different from that of

Luther. The Swiss reformer had lived an active life, had fought as a mercenary soldier in Italian wars, and had acquired practical political experience in the city government of Zurich. These differences in background were bound to make themselves felt when Zwingli began to preach the reformed faith in Zurich (1519), and they were further enhanced by another important factor. Zwingli was a Christian Humanist, and as such he demanded not only that certainty of salvation which came with a faith found, but intellectual certainty as well. In his book on true and false religion (*De Vera et Falsa Religione*, 1525), he set forth his interpretation of Protestantism. One is immediately impressed with the greater rationalism of Zwingli's religious thought, well reflected in his attitude toward church ceremonial. For Luther, baptism and communion were a sanctification through faith, but for Zwingli they were merely external signs of affiliation with the Church. The communion was a memorial service, in contrast to the mystical presence of Christ's blood and body which Luther had found in the sacrament. It was on this doctrine that the conference at Marburg foundered. The disagreement on communion symbolized the profound theological difference between Luther and the Humanist reformer.

For Luther, justification by faith had meant that man's life remained one of penance, that faith was God's free gift, which does not essentially change man's character or free him from the imputation of sin. But for Zwingli justification by faith did free man from the *necessity* of sinning, and he could now, freely and without constraint, fulfill God's will. Zwingli supposed a predisposition to virtue in man, a goodness which originated with God but nevertheless existed in humans. Unlike Luther, Zwingli the Humanist placed great emphasis on man's virtue and on man's will. The damned were only those who, having heard the word of God, refused to follow it.

In this manner Zwingli stressed God's promise of

redemption rather than man's sinful nature. In common with other Humanists, he believed in man's ability to attain truth and faith through education. The instrument of education was the law of God as enshrined in the Bible. Thus, Zwingli rejected everything which could not be found in the Bible. He was a "fundamentalist," and because of this his services consisted simply of readings from the Bible, a sermon, and distribution of the bread and wine. Moreover, laymen could conduct religious services as well as any minister, and Zwingli instituted exercises to train laymen in the art of preaching. These "prophesyings" were taken over by other Protestant sects, and in England they became one of the chief means by which the Puritans harried the Anglican Church of Queen Elizabeth.

How was man to show that he had realized the inherent goodness of his nature, and had received education in the Word of God? He must prove himself through the holiness of his life. It was in this spirit that Zwingli formed in Zurich a board for moral discipline, composed of the clergy, the magistrates, and two elders of the Church. He drew up a list of sins to be punished by excommunication from the society of Christians—a list which included theft, unchastity, perjury, avarice, usury, and fraud. This discipline was to educate man to live according to the Word of God, to aid him in attaining a goal which, once he had found faith, was within his reach. This discipline also differentiated between the saved and those who, by their refusal to follow God's commandments, had shown that they were damned. Both clerics and lay magistrates sat on the board for discipline, a fact which illustrated the fusion of Church and State which Zwingli desired. He became the political as well as the ecclesiastical leader of Zurich; his background in practical statesmanship made him reject a separation between Church and State such as Luther had desired. He everywhere minimized the distinction between ministers and laymen. For him the Church tended to be the community of the faithful, an idea which associated him in the minds of many with the Anabaptists, for whom the Church also consisted of the company of the elect. But, although he was often accused of following their examples, the rationalism of his theology actually placed him outside the Anabaptist camp.

The future influence of Zwingli was based on his concept of church organization, especially on the stress upon ecclesiastical discipline. Bucer in Strassburg and Calvin in Geneva adopted a similar view of church discipline, but they did not fuse State and Church. Bucer envisaged an autonomous Church, having sole jurisdiction over the moral and religious life of its members, and Calvin was to follow Bucer's example. But the political consequences of Zwinglian Reformation are also worthy of note, for they determined the future of Switzerland and thus influenced the position of the city of Geneva, which Calvin was to make the "Rome of Protestantism."

Switzerland was a network of small states or cantons, loosely federated, each one ruled in a more or less democratic fashion. In Zurich, the citizens espoused Zwingli's cause, and his victory in that canton was soon assured (1523). But not all of the Swiss cantons followed in Zurich's footsteps, despite Zwingli's repeated attempts to win them over. His bid for support was resented as a move toward greater centralization within the Swiss federation. The important cantons of Bern and Basel, while favorably inclined toward reform, were not ready to go over to Zwingli's cause and to risk domination by Zurich. The powerful cantons which had formed the original nucleus of the Swiss Confederation (Urkantone), Luzern, Freiburg, Zug, and Unterwalden, remained militantly Catholic. Zwingli's political views helped to keep them in opposition to reform, for the leader of Zurich advocated an end to the recruiting of mercenary soldiers in Switzerland, a plan which sprang out of his own experience as a mercenary in the Italian wars. These cantons, however, were poor farming areas and a military career offered the only chance of outside income for young men. Many availed themselves of this opportunity and swelled the armies of both sides in the wars of Charles V. Thus Zwingli's patriotism presented a threat to the economic life of the inhabitants of the Urkantone and was a considerable factor in their opposition to Zurich Protestantism.

The Urkantone received active support from neighboring Austria, which had no wish to see a centralized and powerful Swiss state menacing its flank. A showdown within the confederation was inevitable. The first victory belonged to Zurich (1529), but the success of that powerful canton only served to spur on the other cities and states of the confederation to increased resistance. Both Bern and Basel were violently opposed to domination by Zurich, and Austria now increased its support of the Catholic cantons. Zwingli could not look to Germany for support. The Schmalkaldic League was purely Lutheran in character, and ever since the Marburg Colloquy, a *rapprochement* between Luther and the Swiss reformer was out of the question. Thus Zurich was defeated in the second and decisive trial of strength. At the battle of Kappel (1531), Zwingli, who had accompanied the army of Zurich as military chaplain, was killed and his body hung from a gibbet.

The battle of Kappel did not entail the end of Protestantism in Switzerland, though it meant that one common religion within the Swiss Confederation was impossible. Zurich, Basel, and Bern remained Protestant, and the latter two cantons became increasingly firm in their faith. In Zurich, the able Heinrich Bullinger became Zwingli's successor. The success of the Reformation in the west Swiss canton of Geneva was largely due to this background of internecine strife in the confederation, as well as to the fact that through this strife, the virtual independence of the several cantons was assured and any trend toward centralization checked.

By the time of the battle of Kappel, the influence of Zwingli had spread beyond Switzerland. The Swiss reform movement had gained support in the valley of the Rhine, and had found a new environment in one of the chief cities of that valley—Strassburg. There the Swiss Reformation gained a considerable following and liturgical reform was accomplished only two years after Zurich had shown the way (1525). But the Protestantism of Strassburg was not to be a mere imitation of Zurich, for the Rhineland soon found a leader who has a place of his own in any history of the Reformation. Martin Bucer was the great peacemaker of the Reformation, and his talent for compromise carried his influence far beyond the valley of the Rhine. However, that influence was not confined to a search for Protestant unity, but had important theological and political consequences as well.

Martin Bucer

Just as Zwingli had been awakened to active interest in the reform movement through the inspiration of Martin Luther, so too had Martin Bucer. Like Luther, the leader of Strassburg reform had been a monk. Before breaking with the established Church, he had left his Dominican monastery and had entered the secular clergy. It was as a chaplain that he attached himself to Franz von Sickingen and became involved in the debacle of the Trier campaign. Unlike Hutten, he did not go into exile, but instead completed his severance from the Church through marriage (1522). By the time of Bucer's arrival in Strassburg (1523), the city had already become one of the chief centers of Protestantism. Due to the political genius of the chief magistrate, Jacob Sturm, Strassburg's importance in the empire was altogether out of proportion to its economic or political power. The theologians of Strassburg had fathered an intellectual renaissance, symbolized by the opening of the Academy in the very year of Bucer's arrival. Bucer was not the only divine for whom Strassburg was to become a place of refuge. There was a tolerant atmosphere in the city, a moderation in all things religious, and a reluctance to enter the battlefield of rival theologies. This conservative moderation meant that Strassburg was well fitted to become the base for Bucer's attempts to win Protestant unity, but it also meant that the city became a harbor for Protestant sects not tolerated elsewhere. Because the supremacy of Zwinglian Protestantism in Strassburg preceded Bucer's arrival, there was even some official sympathy for Anabaptist views, for both creeds shared the belief in a Church defined as consisting of those who had found faith. This situation within Strassburg determined much of Bucer's theological development, for he immediately became involved in a struggle for power with the Anabaptists. Bucer won the fight (1527), and by the time John Calvin came to Strassburg (1538), he was the ecclesiastical leader of the city and had developed a theological viewpoint of his own.

In opposition to Anabaptist beliefs, Martin Bucer stressed man's predestination by God to salvation or damnation; no human could believe himself saved by the certainty of his faith. The Church was not merely a company of "saints," as the Anabaptists believed, but instead embraced all men. There were not two churches, one for those who have received baptism as Christians and another for the "elect," but only one Church, whose spiritual mission manifested itself on earth. This Church was a divine institution to which God had given a task, and no sect had the right to separate itself from this Christian Church on earth. Because the Church had a mission to fulfill, Bucer, like Zwingli, stressed ecclesiastical discipline and the use of excommunication. The Church's duty was partly social in character; one of Bucer's first acts in Strassburg was to reorganize the program of poor relief. But the ideal of education was also present. Bucer considered the building of schools and academies of great importance, especially for the training of ministers. However, the main task of the Church was to call together the faithful through the preaching of the Word, and to expound God's commandments.

Bucer's theological views were important, but of equal significance for the future was the relationship between Church and State which Bucer formulated from this theology. He made the Church an independent power standing beside the State. True, it was the State's duty to provide qualified preachers, but this was a service to the Church, and was not supposed to mean a trend toward State control. For the Church was the custodian of God's word, a decisive concept in a Christian society. Unlike Zwingli's organization, therefore, a board to enforce moral discipline should be composed solely of clerics, and only the Church should have jurisdiction over the weapon of excommunication. This ideal Bucer was not able to realize fully in Strassburg, where Sturm had no wish to see the civil authority weakened by having at its side an equal, if not superior, Church. But Bucer did manage to realize the Christian state in Hesse, where the elector invited him to reorganize Hessian ecclesiastical institutions. Here we find a Church-State relationship which was to become the ideal of the Calvinist Church.

With Bucer, the Reformation became an emancipation of the Church from the State, rather than its subjugation to temporal authority. On such central theological points as the communion service, he changed his mind several times in his role as the peacemaker among the reformers. In the end, he agreed with Luther's point of view as to the presence of Christ in the sacrament. The fact that Bucer seems to have given in to Luther on this vital point has served to diminish his theological stature for historians, and to obscure his real contribution. Bucer's political failures had the same effect on his future reputation. He was unable to achieve Protestant unity and he was, in the end, to fail even in Strassburg.

Charles V's victories over the League of Schmalkalden imperiled the independence of Strassburg and the cause of the Reformation within the city. The Interim (1548), which Charles proclaimed after his victory, forced the princes and the cities of the empire to adopt a religious program essentially Catholic in character. Jacob Sturm was successful in persuading the city council of Strassburg to accept the Interim in order to save the city from destruction. Bucer was unwilling to go along; his idea of concession did not extend to the adoption of a predominantly Catholic religious program. Though Sturm humbled himself and the city before the victorious emperor, he was ultimately successful in preserving not only the independence of Strassburg, but also in maintaining the Protestant faith alongside a restored Catholicism. Bucer, on the other hand, was given leave by the city council to accept an invitation to teach in England. Thus he never achieved control over the city; the magistrates retained the real power, which thwarted the fruition of his ideals of Church-State relationships. In the end they politely exiled the reformer.

During this struggle within Strassburg, Bucer further developed his political theories, which were already spelled out in his *Commentary on St. Matthew* (1527). Bucer did not depart from Luther's idea that a Christian has to regard existing laws and rulers as willed by God. But for the citizen of Strassburg, this maxim was capable of creating opposite results. Not only the emperor, but also the authorities in self-governing cities were instituted directly by God as magistrates. The same held true for all the German princely states. Here the demand of religion to preserve the order established by God implied the conservation of political variety within the empire. Viewed in this light, inferior authorities gained a new strength, a new spiritual dignity. The early Jewish state in the Old Testament proved that God did not want an unlimited absolutism. Did God not give to His people an absolute ruler (Saul) only in His wrath? Given Bucer's political ideals with their source in religious conviction, it becomes obvious why he could not assent to the Interim, which was imposed by an emperor wanting absolute authority and encroaching upon the power of God-appointed "inferior" magistrates. Hans Baron has further shown that the direct successor to this mode of political thought was John Calvin. He translated the political ideas of Bucer into the language of Western Europe. Here, not the city councils or the princes, but parliaments and estates took the place of "inferior" magistrates, and Calvin gave these bodies a status which enabled them to oppose any absolute monarch hostile to their theology.

The struggles in Strassburg were not to be Bucer's last efforts to realize his ideals. He tried to persuade the young and pious King Edward VI of England to accept his plans for the Church, and in order to convince the monarch, he set them down plainly in his book, *De Regno Christi* (1551). Yet Edward proved unable to follow the advice of the aged Protestant leader. Young and mortally ill, he was a tool in the hands of rival noble factions.

Bucer's lasting contribution to Protestantism depends largely on the influence he exercised upon Calvin. There can be little doubt about the importance of his political theories for the development of Calvin, but there is room for dispute about his direct theological influence. Ideas of predestination and the role of the Church on earth can be found in St. Augustine, and it is from this source that Bucer took his views. As the Bishop of Hippo fought against the Donatist heresy, so Bucer fought against the Anabaptists. The writings of the saint were relevant to the situation of the reformer. Calvin may well have received his ideas independently by reading *The City of God,* and Bucer's influence may have been only secondary in character. Even so, his influence was of great importance; Calvin's *Institutes* shows the effect which Bucer's writings and personality had on the French reformer. It was after his sojourn in Strassburg that Calvin began to stress predestination and, above all, the role of the Church on earth. Such signs of Bucer's influence are too strong to be ignored, even if St. Augustine was the common inspiration for both reformers. Bucer's failure to realize and to maintain his form of Protestantism is, therefore, not as important as the way in which he was able to transmit his ideas to the world through Calvinism. For Calvin's Protestantism was to be successful and was to spread not only through Europe but to the New World as well.

John Calvin

Years of Wandering. The personality of John Calvin was formed by an environment and a training quite different from that of Martin Luther. He was not educated against a background of popular piety, and he did not reach maturity in the cell of a monk. Instead, Calvin was the product of an urban culture and of the best Humanist and judicial training which France had to offer. His mother, however, was a pious woman, and under her influence he at first began an ecclesiastical career which led to study at the College of Montaigu, part of the Sorbonne, in Paris. The College of Montaigu was dedicated to the defense of orthodoxy as opposed to the ideas of Martin Luther. It was here that Calvin must have experienced his first contact with Protestantism and, more important, with the theological thought of Occam and Duns Scotus. Like Luther at Erfurt, Calvin was impressed with the absolute power of God which this theology tended to stress. But, unlike Luther, this did not produce in Calvin a spiritual crisis leading to a break with established ecclesiastical forms. With the death of his mother, his father's influence prevailed, and Calvin turned from theology to law as an avenue of advancement to worldly power and riches.

He studied under the legal masters at Orléans and Bourges, and at the latter University came into contact with the Italian Humanist Alciat, who infused in his student a love of good writing and precise Latin. This training helped Calvin to become one of the foremost prose writers and Latinists of his era. But more than this, Calvin became seriously interested in Humanism, an interest already present by the time he left Paris. Italian Humanism and, above all, the revived ideas of the Stoics left an imprint on his thought. Calvin's concept of a law of nature and of the natural unity of human society can be traced to Seneca, whose discourse on mercy Calvin edited (1532). Moreover, the Stoic idea of fate could easily be transformed into the concept of predestination. Through Humanist learning, he also came into contact with the Latin writings of the early Church, especially with St. Augustine's *City of God.* It is important to realize, however, that Calvin never joined the main stream of Christian Humanism; the mild mysticism of his countryman Lefèvre had no influence upon Calvin's Humanist thought. Calvin's theology had more in common with Luther than with the Christian Humanists, and he denounced Zwingli for his emphasis upon man's power of will and inherent goodness.

In 1533 Calvin joined for the first time the partisans of church reform. It seemed in that year that Francis I would support the reforming party. Margaret of Navarre, long a supporter of Christian Humanism, had persuaded her brother to allow the open preaching of reformist sermons at the royal palace. The orthodox resistance of the Sorbonne to any kind of change appeared to be waning, and even the new rector, Nicholas Cop, advocated gradual reforms within the framework of the Church. Calvin was a close friend of Cop and is known to have been the ghost writer of the rector's inaugural address. However, Francis I disappointed the reformers. In October of the next year (1534), the appearance in the palace of proclamations

John Calvin. *(Radio Times Hulton Picture Library)*

against the Catholic Mass gave Francis an opportunity to reverse his stand. He had never wished to see a fundamental change in a Church he already controlled through ecclesiastical appointments. Public order seemed menaced by a religious radicalism which threatened to escape royal control. Nicholas Cop, Lefèvre and Calvin were accused of being "Lutherans" and had to flee the country. Calvin's days of Humanist study were past, though he never ceased to long for a return of times conducive to learning and quiet reflection. Like Cop, the younger man fled to Basel. By that time, his basic ideas appear to have been fully formed. In the year after the affair of the proclamations, he published the first edition of his *Institutes of a Christian Religion* (1536). With this book began the religious mission of John Calvin.

His years of wandering were not over; from Basel he went to Italy in order to seek his fortune at the court of Ferrara. Here Calvin found little understanding, and his thoughts now turned to Strassburg, where his friend Bucer desired his presence. He returned for a brief and secret visit to France, intending to continue later to Strassburg. The wars between Francis I and Charles V forced a revision of his plan because of the closing of the frontier between France and the empire. Thus Calvin had to make a detour via Geneva, where his friend William Farel was struggling to introduce reform. In this way Calvin became acquainted with the city which was to become his home, and which he was to make famous throughout Europe. Strassburg had to wait; there was work to be done in Geneva.

Salvation by Faith. In France, Calvin was accused of being a "Lutheran," and Luther's influence upon him cannot be discounted. Like Luther, Calvin developed his thought around the justification of sinful man through the mediation of Christ. The differences between Calvin and Luther lay in their concepts of the relationship between Christ and the believer. For

Luther, salvation was by faith alone. For Calvin, the
power of God and the irremediable sinfulness of man
modified this concept.

God is the creator and sovereign governor of the
world. The greatest achievement of His creation is man
himself. Adam's betrayal of God's trust in him was
perfidy of the highest degree, for Adam was the goal
and the end of all God's strivings. Thus original sin
was of central importance in Calvin's theology. Through
original sin man became a perpetual sinner. How, then,
does God communicate with His fallen creatures?

The Bible tells us all we can know about God. But
the Bible alone is not enough, for the Word cannot be
understood except by those who have faith. The purpose of Biblical study is to know Christ, without whom
nothing about God can ever be known by mortals.
The spirit of Christ can be found in the Old as well
as in the New Testament, for God's purpose is in-
divisible and He cannot have said one thing in the
Old Testament and another in the New. Thus, the
Old Testament is a preparation for the coming of
Christ, and while the particular ceremonial and judicial
laws of the people of Israel have no longer any validity,
the moral directives of the Old Testament are in perpetual force. Calvin's emphasis upon the validity of
the stern moral commandments of the Old Testament
did not mean that Christ was neglected; indeed he oc-
cupies a central position in God's relations with man.
Christ is the mediator who made salvation possible for
fallen man, and who testified to God's great goodness
by his meditation. As one writer put it in the next
century: "We are ignorant clients, God is a skillful
judge, Christ is our advocate to plead our cause for
us." Calvin does not allow a separation between God
and Christ. Christ himself is Divine, and God cannot
be found except through Christ. Man's disobedience,
which was the cause of his fall, must now be replaced
by an obedience to Christ, in order to satisfy God's
strict justice.

Is salvation, then, attained solely through faith in God through Christ? Here Calvin's concept of God as sole sovereign enters. For faith is a gift of God, exclusive to those whom He has freely elected to salvation through the mediation of Christ. It is here that the idea of predestination comes to be of importance. Predestination is the primeval judgment of God, by which He has determined each man's fate; some He has called, through Christ, to salvation, and others to eternal damnation. To Calvin, this did not entail disquietude of soul, for communion with Christ meant certainty of election. The faithful who are united with Christ have no cause to speculate about their election to salvation. This predestination is not the stern doctrine of God's wrath which it tended to become in later Puritanism.

How do the "saints" give testimony of their election? By their faith, which partly manifests itself in the doing of good works. Calvin was careful to avoid deifying his saints, as the Anabaptists tended to do. Even the works of the elect can be faulty, for no human can ever aspire to perfection. Because they are far from the perfection of Christ, the lives of the elect must be lived in penance. Thus, those whom God has elected must prepare themselves for a hard, laborious existence, full of work and infinite varieties of evil. Life is a struggle against suffering and tribulation, and the Christian must carry his cross in this world, while contemplating the life to come. But there is also a rejection of this world implied in Calvin's thought, for by becoming regenerated, we are freed from the ambitions and involvements of mundane life in order to serve Christ more effectively. Thus, asceticism and the rejection of worldly concerns combined with the frugal life and the continued struggle against evil to form the pattern for Calvinist living.

God, Calvin wrote, wants the world to be a theater for His glory. The elect, however, were not the only actors on this stage; there were also the reprobates

who were predestined to damnation. It was impossible
to establish outward signs of inward grace; therefore,
it was difficult to distinguish between the reprobate and
the elect on earth. There were only a few cases, such
as those of outright heretics, where such a distinction
could be clearly made. In the last resort, election or
reprobation was written in the conscience of the individual concerned. Who can express man's horror
better than himself: "He goeth through a thousand
deaths and cannot die." The saint is a man who lives
a dedicated, frugal, industrious life, and, thus fortified
with a good conscience, battles the forces of evil both
in this world and in his own imperfect soul. It is in
later Calvinism that a clear conscience tends to become self-righteousness, and a life of penitence is rewarded by riches; the same qualities which the "saints"
were to possess also proved congenial to middle-class
industry and acquisitiveness. For Calvin, such a reading of his doctrines would have been repugnant, for
the only sign of God's free grace given through Christ
was in the soul, and no outward signs of inward grace
could exist in the theater of the world, where only
divinity meant perfection.

The Church. Because no distinction can be made between the elect and the reprobate, the Church must
include both. Inasmuch as we are far from perfect, we
need external means through which faith can be furthered within us, and God has instituted the Church
in order to aid our infirmities. It is thus God's instrument to aid our sanctification. At the same time, the
Church is the product of the contact between God and
man, renewed through the coming of Christ. Equally
with Bucer, Calvin emphasized a church organization
independent of the whim of temporal power. The
church must be based upon the precepts of Christ, free
to fulfill its task on earth.

Preaching the Word was one task of **the Church.**

Individual reading of the Bible was not enough; Calvin's legal training seems to display itself in his contention that man needs guidance in order to read the Scriptures correctly. To provide that guidance, he wrote his *Institutes of the Christian Religion,* and revised them from time to time in order to develop more completely parts of his theology. Thus the concepts of the Church and of predestination were only sketchily treated in the first edition (1536), but more fully discussed in the edition which was published after his sojourn in Strassburg (1539); his political ideas were most fully developed in the last edition of this great work (1559). The Church was still necessary for the preaching and teaching of the Word—the work of pastors and doctors respectively. Their fitness for office was seen by the spirit of Christ working within them, but also by community election. Calvin, his aristocratic tendencies already in evidence, thought of this election as the approbation by the community of men picked by the other pastors, doctors, and magistrates. To these preachers and teachers of the Word, Calvin added other officers of the Church. The principal function of the elders was to maintain the ecclesiastical discipline. They were also elected by the people, as were the deacons, whose work consisted of taking care of the poor and the sick. These four categories of officials, which were modeled on Strassburg practice, assured the independent functioning of the Church in the vital areas of of preaching, administering communion, maintaining discipline, and dispensing charity.

The Church embraced all Christians in its function of channeling their thoughts and actions communally toward Christ. Individualism was not possible among those for whom obedience to Christ was the first commandment. Thus the Church was responsible for the poor and the sick. Poverty and reprobation had not yet come to mean the same thing; Calvin's Church stressed collective responsibility. In the last resort, the

Church was responsible to Christ, and it is here that ecclesiastical discipline enters. The Church was a divine institution; therefore, any action against it was also an attack on the divinity of Christ. Disorder and scandal could not be tolerated either in matters of doctrine or in the conduct of Christians. Men are prone to sin, follow bad examples, and are led astray. But Calvin's discipline was not merely repressive or designed for the maintenance of order. It was, above all, educational and a part of the cure of souls. Those chastised by the Church were humbled in their sins and thereby led more quickly to mend their way of life and to purify their souls. This discipline is not the essence of Calvin's concept of a Church, but a defensive measure against those who would attack Christ, and an educational measure to lead men to the realization of faith. Nor can discipline mean reprobation (except in the case of stubborn heretics), for who on earth knows the number of the elect?

The relations between Church and State in Calvinism have often been described as those of a "theocracy," a domination of the State by the Church. However, what Calvin, like Bucer, envisaged, was not domination, but the collaboration of temporal and spiritual authorities. Ecclesiastical jurisdiction pertains solely to the Church, as had been the case in medieval canon law. The Church is an organization of eternal validity, and for Calvin political authority was a temporal and ephemeral affair outside the sphere of Christ's principal concern. Yet magistrates were Christians, and as such were under the jurisdiction of the Church as well as under their own temporal justice. Moreover, if there was scandal in the Church and nothing was done about it, the magistrate should come to the Church's aid. Conversely, the Church should see to it that the magistrates were conversant with the Word of God, and that civil legislation did not run contrary to God's law. Church and State were not rivals for supreme power,

yet it is easy to see how at a later date theocratic ideas
could develop. What if the magistrate did not heed the
Word? In the last resort, the Church of Christ was
superior to any temporal authority.

Calvin dedicated his *Institutes* to Francis I in the
hope that he would become a "Christian" king. It surely never crossed his mind that the ruler might be
frightened away from the faith by fear of church domination. But by the time of the last edition of the
Institutes (1559), Calvin had been disillusioned by
monarchs. He now followed Bucer's path by endowing
the minor magistrates with powers to limit the absolutism of rulers. He spoke not only as a citizen of the
city-state of Geneva, but deduced his conclusions from
his theology. If the preservation of the sovereignty of
God is the center of faith, then it becomes an offense
against God to give unlimited power to any earthly
creature, imperfect by his very nature. Legal limitations upon the ruler were made a requirement of
religion. Moreover, hereditary succession impaired
God's powers of selection; thus elective government, as
practiced in the Church, was superior to hereditary
kingship. The political resistance which Calvinism encountered in France and the other nation-states made
Calvin formulate revolutionary conclusions from his
theology. However much they fit into the pattern of his
thought, they cannot be found in his earlier writings.
By 1559, Calvin had assumed a position which gave
support to the aims of the advocates of constitutional
government as opposed to royal absolutism—aims which
furthered the ambitions of the "outs" throughout
Europe. The middle classes in the cities, the small nobility in France, and the factious nobles of Scotland could
find more than spiritual solace in Calvinism. Although
on the face of it Calvin's idea of a Church had much
in common with that of Luther, his emphasis on church
organization and his more concrete ideas on collaboration between Church and magistrate ended by appeal-

ing to large sections of the population, for whom election through faith seemed also to promise riches and political power.

The Conquest of Geneva. In Geneva, John Calvin found a city whose history had been shaped by a long struggle to maintain its civic privileges. The right to elect magistrates (syndics) and representative councils was jealously guarded. The intensity of the devotion shown in preserving these rights was furthered by the ambitions of neighboring states, who cast covetous eyes on the strategically located city. The powerful neighbors of Geneva were the duke of Savoy to the south and the Swiss canton of Bern to the east. The adoption of the Genevan Reformation was due to the menace from Savoy, and the course of the reform was influenced by the ambitions of Bern. The immediate menace to independence came from the duke of Savoy, who attempted to obtain control through the appointment of the bishop of Geneva, traditionally the protector of the city. Geneva looked for allies, and found them in the Catholic canton of Freiburg, as well as in Protestant Bern.

This alliance accomplished its immediate end. The bishop fled Geneva (1533) and joined forces with Savoy in order to bring the city to heel. With the aid of Freiburg and Bern, the army of Savoy was defeated (1535). But this victory proved only the beginning of Geneva's problems. The war had been waged for the sake of political freedom, but religious issues could not be ignored. The failure of the bishop had been a blow to Catholic prestige in Geneva, and powerful Bern was pressing for Protestant reform in order to get the city within its grasp. However, Freiburg, the other ally, was opposed to such a policy, and within Geneva it is estimated that, as late as 1534, two thirds of the inhabitants were Catholic in sentiment. This was the situation when Bern sent William Farel to the city to preach the evangelical faith.

It was Farel who started the Reformation in Geneva. Without his accomplishments, those of Calvin would have been impossible. In his work, Farel was helped by the realization on the part of many powerful Genevan families that the Bern alliance was a better guarantee against continued pressure from Savoy than a compact with the weaker Catholic Freiburg. Moreover, in the minds of many, Savoy and Catholicism were identified and equally branded as enemies of civic liberties. The alliance with Freiburg was broken (1535), and that canton now allied itself with Savoy against Geneva. Bern was now Geneva's greatest hope, and reformation became an accomplished fact (1536); Farel's mission seemed destined to be successful. Yet the Reformation came to Geneva as a by-product of political desires rather than as a result of theological conviction. This was shown again when Bern proceeded to demand the overlordship of the city as the price of its support. Geneva indignantly rejected this demand; they had fought Savoy "not because we had the intention of making the city subject to any power, but because we wished the poor city which had warred and suffered so much to have its liberty." Calvin was soon to realize that this concept of liberty was a political one and that it would oppose a reformation which would detract from the power and independence of civil authority.

Though Bern's bid for domination had been rejected, relations between the two cities continued to be close; the Reformation in that city attracted the authorities of Geneva. Bern followed Zwinglian church organization; Church and State were fused, and the civil authorities also had ecclesiastical powers. The Genevan councils followed this pattern when the Reformation was accepted, making themselves arbiters in all religious matters. Genevans thought the expulsion of nuns, priests, and bishops had ended the matter, and that no basic theological transformation was needed or desirable. There was no organized church;

the councils continued to control ecclesiastical property, to hire and dismiss ministers, and to pass any religious legislation they saw fit. This was the situation when Calvin entered Geneva, and it was Farel's sense of futility which made him plead with Calvin to aid him in his efforts. For though Farel had his Reformation, he also desired more positive church organization accompanied by theological change. This not only meant opposition from within Geneva, but also conflict with Bern, which desired the adoption of its type of Protestantism in the neighboring city.

Who, then, held the real power in Geneva? Not the people, for the city was controlled by an oligarchy; out of a population of 13,000, only about 1500 of the more wealthy citizens had the power to vote. These citizens were usually members of the chief families of the town. There were two principal city councils: the Little Council of twenty-five members, and the Big Council of two hundred. There was also a council of all citizens, which elected four syndics each year and sanctioned treaties and alliances. But this council was declining in importance. The syndics were usually chosen from a list drawn up by the council of the two hundred; moreover, there was a tendency toward concentration of power within the councils, for we find the same prominent men obtaining positions of trust and responsibility year after year. The issues within the city were thus decided among the powerful families, and here the real power within Geneva was to be found. It was under these conditions that Calvin had to push through his ecclesiastical reforms.

Calvin began to do this the very year of his arrival (1536). He submitted to the councils articles of faith which, while including his basic theological ideals, did not derogate from the councils' final authority over all ecclesiastical matters. Moreover, as Calvin pointed out, such articles of faith would mean a greater stability in the city and therefore would strengthen the hands of authority. Emboldened by the acceptance of his articles,

Calvin submitted a confession of faith (1537) to which all Genevans were to swear public allegiance. This brought on a crisis, for it forced Calvinism upon all inhabitants of the city, and bound them to the reformer's ideas of church discipline.

This crisis made again evident the extent to which Protestantism had been adopted for political reasons; even in the adoption of the articles of faith, this had been a major consideration. Many had gone along with Calvin because his Protestantism, differing from that of Bern, meant greater municipal independence, while his ideas of discipline meant personal security by keeping the populace under control and surveillance. Now powerful elements in the city regarded Calvinism as a new despotism, as foreign as that of Savoy or Bern. Moreover, there was still Catholic sentiment in Geneva, which did not want the issue joined. As a result, Calvin's supporters on the councils were voted out of office, and his opponents attained political power. Ministers were warned not to mix in politics, but to stick to the gospel. Geneva returned to the concept of a State-dominated Church. To this, Calvin could never consent, and both he and Farel were asked to leave the city on three days' notice (1538).

It seemed as though Calvin's mission had failed. The reformer went to Strassburg, belatedly fulfilling his wish to settle in Bucer's city. But three years later he was recalled to the town he had left with such distaste. Once again it was politics which led to Calvin's return. The party which had opposed him used its new power arbitrarily. It ruthlessly dismissed from office all his former supporters, and thus alienated many prominent families. The severities of Calvin's enemies seemed no better, indeed they seemed worse, than those proposed by Calvin himself. Meanwhile Calvin's rising prestige in the Protestant world added to the feeling of loss which his friends claimed the city had sustained by his departure. What finally discredited the party in power, however, was its consent to a treaty with Bern which abandoned Genevan claims to disputed territories. Municipal pride and hostility toward foreign encroachment were aroused, and it was the party of Calvin's friends which now came to power (1540). Calvin re-entered the city the next year (1541), requesting immediate assistance in drawing up a constitution for the Genevan Church. Calvin's work at Geneva had begun afresh; it lasted the rest of his life.

The Genevan Church. The constitution which Calvin drew up for the Church of Geneva had an importance far beyond the boundaries of that city. The Calvinist churches of France, the Netherlands, Germany, and Scotland attempted to preserve the fundamental ideals of the *Ordonnances Ecclésiastiques* (1541). They were the practical application of the theology of the *Institutes.* The central organism of the church was the consistory. This body was composed of ministers and of a dozen members of the councils co-opted by the clergy. The consistory was charged with the maintenance of church discipline, and thus became the most controversial body in the Calvinist Church. Its members applied censure or excommunication against those inhabitants of the city who had violated dogma or morality. They had ecclesiastical jurisdiction and thus symbolized the autonomy of the church which Calvin desired. But that autonomy was never complete. Despite Calvin's domination of the city, the councils refused to allow excommunication except with their express consent. It was not until four years after the *Ordonnances* that Calvin obtained the councils' consent to have excommunication pronounced before the whole community; until that time the civil authorities had feared such publicity. If ordinary inhabitants could benefit from church discipline, the oligarchy wanted to keep the church from full use of this powerful weapon.

The "Venerable Company of Pastors" was a less controversial body. It was the gathering of all the ministers of the city to discuss and prepare legislation for the consideration of the consistory. Laymen were represented by twelve elders chosen by the councils. This company also approved the appointment of teachers and licensed ministers. The basis of the ecclesiastical organization was the four orders of spiritual office which Calvin had adopted from Strassburg. These were, for the most part, elected by their congregations.

This was the framework with which Calvin proceeded to reform Geneva. While ecclesiastical discipline was not the essence of his theology, in the Genevan situation it assumed great importance. The city was divided into parishes, and provision was made for systematic worship and education in each. Two members of the consistory, accompanied by the minister, made regular rounds of each parish, in order that "their eyes might be on the people." The transgressor was escorted to the consistory which met once each week for trial. Public penance, fines, public apology were the punishments for minor offenses. This strict discipline proved an educational success. A pleasure-loving, wealthy city was transformed into a theater for the glory of God. Profane theatrical plays were forbidden, and religious plays took their places. Inns were closed and hostels substituted. In the hostels, where the innkeepers were under strict surveillance, the only distraction allowed was the reading of the Bible in French. But this innovation proved too much of a change and lasted only a month. The same can be said for the campaign against Christian names which were not of Biblical origin. Under mounting popular protest this campaign was abandoned after a trial run of several years' duration. There was a limit, even, to the enforcement of church discipline. Yet the consistory probed into every part of the lives of parishioners. Dancing, card playing, and playing bowls at Easter led to prison. One young woman who sang profane songs was banished, and another, who sang them to Psalm tunes, was scourged.

Powerful members of the oligarchy were not safe from punishment. One member of the Little Council,

Pierre Ameaux, had been heard to say that Calvin was a bad man, a preacher of wrong doctrine; the council asked Ameaux to retract, kneeling, in front of the council of two hundred. But for Calvin this was not enough. Ameaux had to walk through town, clad only in a shirt, with a flaming torch in his hand (1546). One can imagine the impression produced upon the people by this punishment. Here was a member of the ruling class of the city, humbled for having questioned the authority of Calvin. The reformer himself held no outstanding position, he was only a member of the consistory and a minister at the Church of St. Pierre.

Exasperation with this strict discipline was bound to make itself felt. Even members of powerful families who had supported the reformer began to question the competence of the consistory. It seemed to lead toward a theocracy. Yet Calvin himself was always careful not to interfere with purely civil concerns. Moreover, he had not achieved complete church autonomy; excommunication was, in the last resort, the responsibility of the councils, and not that of the church. This did not prevent an attempt by a powerful faction again to drive Calvin out of the city.

The years 1551 to 1555 were years of decision. Political opposition to Calvin fused with theological opposition. The attack by Hieronymous Bolsec upon Calvin's ideas of predestination (1551) became the rallying point of the reformer's enemies. They succeeded in having the civil authorities take the lead in the interrogation of Bolsec, and in requesting opinions from other Swiss churches. The ministers of the city favored excommunication, but the magistrates substituted perpetual banishment. Here the councils had interfered in purely church business, and had refused to follow the advice of the clergy. The opposition had publicly challenged the right of the consistory to have any say in the matter of excommunication. Calvin himself had pursued a moderate course, advocating banishment. But Bolsec saw in Calvin the root of his troubles, and published

a biography of the reformer (1577), which for two centuries provided the inspiration for anti-Calvinist polemical writings.

The banishment of Bolsec did not end Calvin's troubles. It was only the prelude to the affair of Servetus (1553). Servetus held that man was an emanation of divinity, an idea which was close to the concept of the Platonists of the Italian Renaissance. He denied eternity to Jesus the son, instead Christ was coterminus with God. A more fundamental attack on all religious orthodoxy could hardly be imagined. His life had not been tranquil, and the fact that he loved a good argument had put him in peril of death several times before he ever reached Geneva. He sought asylum in Italy, and it was on his way to Naples that he passed through the city. He was no stranger to Calvin, who had already written a refutation of his views. Servetus was imprudent enough to make his presence known in Geneva, and Calvin asked for his arrest. Through his contentiousness Servetus made a bad impression on the councils, and Calvin found the civil authorities in complete agreement with his views. The trial and burning of Servetus saw a harmony and cooperation between Church and State which had been absent in Bolsec's case. The burning itself was hardly an extraordinary event. Hundreds of Anabaptists and heretics had been burned in the Protestant world before Servetus. A heretic was a danger to man's soul, and it was considered only right to burn those who killed the soul of man, just as one put to death murderers who killed man's body. Melanchthon expressed his gratitude to Calvin for the act, and the Swiss churches gave unanimous approval.

But collaboration between councils and consistory in the case of Servetus did not suffice to eradicate anti-Calvinist feeling in the city. That same year the magistrates granted to one prominent citizen the right to present himself at communion, an open infraction of Church-State relationships. But Calvin's support was being strengthened by political success. For he was able to get admitted to citizenship the Protestant refugees who began to fill the city. Here was a real and devoted following on which he could count amidst the intrigues of the oligarchy. The number of these new inhabitants in the city rose with great rapidity as the persecution of Calvinists increased in their native countries, and as pilgrims arrived to witness the godly society. There were eighty-one of these citizens on the municipal registers by 1548; eight years later their number had risen above three hundred, and by 1557, after Calvin's final triumph in the city had been assured, they constituted five hundred and eighty-seven souls. Re-enforced by this support, Calvin was able to eliminate his enemies from the councils and to prepare for a decisive victory. He accomplished his aim by ably exploiting a political situation, for Calvin had become an astute politician as a result of his apprenticeship in the municipal politics of Geneva. A harmless riot was magnified by him into an attempted revolution against civil and ecclesiastical authority (1555). The result was that his enemies were banished from the city and complete victory achieved in the same year that Lutheranism was officially recognized in the empire.

Calvin crowned his success by the founding of an academy (1559). Here ministers and scholars were to be educated in the Calvinist faith. It included classes from the secondary school level to training in theology. Its leader was Theodore Béza, Calvin's successor as guide of the Genevan Church. This institution was to influence Protestant academies throughout Europe, as well as the schools of the Jesuits.

This, then, was Calvin's Geneva. It was not the complete kingdom of God on earth which he had envisaged, but there have been few men in history who have had the opportunity of putting their ideas to the test of practice. Calvin's theories had experienced practical realization in Geneva, and that gave them an infectious character they might otherwise have lacked. To Protestants in many other lands, the Swiss city represented the new Jerusalem, the godly society in actual working order.

The Impact of Geneva. It has been said, with some justice, that Calvin constructed a new Catholicism outside the old and in opposition to it. Calvin's relationship to the reformed churches in the West was not unlike that of the pope to the Catholic Church. From his "Rome" on the shores of Lake Leman he organized and controlled the "true" churches in the other nations. His special concern had always been the reformation of France, and the course of that reformation was directed from Geneva.

Calvin unified the diverse attempts at reform in his native country, and gave them a common faith and a common discipline. From small Bible-reading groups in scattered and hostile communities he formed his churches. His first effort was to obtain strict adherence to his theology. He thus fought the influence of those who followed the ideas of Servetus or of Zwingli, as well as the Nicodèmites. This latter movement was especially appealing in a hostile environment, for it believed it proper to adhere to the forms of the traditional faith, while believing in the basic ideas of the Reformation. This compromise appealed to the rich and powerful, various royal officials and merchants, who wanted both peace and salvation. For Calvin this was sheer opportunism; God wants us entirely and not just "in secret." He was successful in defeating this movement (1543), and thereby hammered out well-defined churches which looked to Geneva for help and guidance. Calvin's instruments in controlling the French churches were the ministers. These were elected, according to Calvinist custom, but approbation from Geneva became essential. Calvin regarded France as a missionary province, and from Geneva he sent out ministers in whom he had confidence to make sure his rules were observed. At the same time, he en-

couraged pilgrimages to Geneva by the faithful, in
order that they might get their inspiration from the
source. Such pilgrimages were fraught with danger, for
the French government put every obstacle in the way
of the pilgrims. But this did not mitigate Calvin's attitude; indeed, a visit to Geneva strengthened the believer, for he had to declare himself as one of the
true church, regardless of the dangers involved.

Through discipline Calvin welded together the
French Calvinist or Huguenot Church. Each church
had ministers and elders who together formed the consistory of the individual church. In order to obtain
greater unification there was a regional meeting of
neighboring churches called the colloquy. Each minister of an individual church was also supposed to
receive the approbation of the neighboring congregations, a custom followed later in New England. The
whole province met in the provincial synod and above
that was the national synod itself. It was not until
1559 that Calvin permitted such a national assembly to
meet, and then its first action was to adopt a confession of faith sent from Geneva. At the same time
a common church discipline was adopted, a "guardedly
representative structure," as John T. McNeill has called
it. The elders and deacons were elected in the first instance and then co-opted by the consistory. In the
synods both elders and ministers sat as representatives
of their congregations. Elections by the congregations
were not, however, democratic processes entailing both
nomination of candidates and then their election or
rejection. Instead, the elders and ministers usually put
forward candidates and the congregation signified either
approval or disapproval of them.

The first church had been organized in Paris in
1555, and at the first national synod there were some
fifty churches in attendance. Moreover, members of important noble families, both on the local and national
level, had joined congregations. Given their status in
society, they came to play an important role in the

John Knox Preaching Before the Lords of the Congregation, painting by Sir David Wilkie. (*The Bettmann Archive*)

church, and a man like Gaspard de Coligny became the political leader of the church as a whole. The well-structured organization of the churches made them a viable base of operations in a nation where there were no constitutional means to effect the changes Calvinism desired. In the Religious Wars (1559–1589) the Huguenot Church was to withstand the hard test of survival.

Out of scattered, timid Protestant cells, Calvin had formed a church. Discipline maintained unity of belief and gave a feeling of security to those who might waver in their allegiance. The faithful worked in a hostile environment; their meetings took place at night and guards were posted to give alarm in case of a police raid. What could be greater testimony to Calvin's organization of the Huguenot Church than the fact that this persecuted minority was soon to become strong enough to provide an effective framework in the struggle for political power which marked the French religious wars?

France was Calvin's chief, but by no means only, concern. One year after the meeting of the first French National Synod, the first Calvinist Church was established in Scotland (1560). Calvin's role in the conquest of Scotland was advisory only and he avoided direct interference, for the Scottish Reformation had found a reliable leader in John Knox, who had been minister in the English congregation of Geneva (1553–1555). Knox was able to win adherents among the Scottish nobility, who were opposed to a monarchy closely allied with Catholic France. The Protestant nobles formed a covenant for the establishment of the Word of God in Scotland (1557). By 1560 they had triumphed, after three years of civil strife. The organization of the Scottish Church was similar to that of France. The "colloquy" and the "synod" played important roles, but the emphasis in Scotland was placed on the self-sufficiency of individual congregations, and upon voluntary unions of elders and pastors, which in the organization ranked below the synod. These were the presbyteries from which the Scottish Church was to take its name. Basically, it was another actualization of Calvin's ideal of church government.

Calvin's political theories, as he expressed them in 1559, were to fall on fertile soil in Scotland. The struggle against monarchy made for an appreciation of constitutionalism. But Knox went beyond the Calvinist doctrines of limitations upon the ruler; he advocated the overthrow of the ruler if he refused to support the church. "The common song is that we must obey our kings, be they good or bad, for God has so commanded. . . . But it is no less than blasphemy to say God commanded kings to be obeyed when they command impiety." This was radically different from Luther's interpretation of St. Paul's injunction to obey the powers-that-be, for they are ordained by God. Knox instead stressed the scriptural injunction that wicked men should be cut off without exception. Calvinist ideas of collaboration between Church and State here led to a radicalism which inspired James VI of Scotland to accuse Presbyterian ministers of teaching that kings and princes were natural enemies of the church. These political theories were not confined to Knox, but were adopted wherever Calvinism had to fight against established authority. Thus we find them in the Huguenots' famed *Vindicia Contra Tyrannos* (1579), and in the writings of many English Puritans.

In England, also, Calvin's influence made itself felt, but more indirectly than in Scotland. Many prominent Protestants came under his spell during the reign of the Catholic Queen Mary (1553–1558). Geneva became a natural place of refuge, and these men took home many of Calvin's ideas when they returned to Elizabethan England. English Puritanism was never wholly orthodox. Other influences, such as those of the Rhineland, entered into its making. Not until well after Calvin's death was the first short-lived presbytery established in England (1574). But here, as elsewhere in Europe, Calvin's influence was exercised through his writings, if not directly. As in the case of Luther, astute use of the printing press aided missionary work. Not only were the *Institutes,* the *Catechism,* and his many Biblical commentaries printed, but, like Luther, the French reformer published a Bible—an official version based on authentic texts. It was not the kind of fundamental translation which Luther had produced; its chief novelty was the marginal notes which provided a Calvinist commentary for the reader. This Bible soon displayed Lefèvre's translations in France; Whittingham and his associates fashioned an English translation which was to have great popularity during Elizabeth's reign. It was in order to defeat the popular appeal of the "Geneva" Bible that King James I ordered a new translation. Thus, the Calvinist Bible was indirectly responsible for the "King James version," which has become a literary classic as well as the most used Bible in the English-speaking world.

France, Scotland, and England do not exhaust the story of Calvin's influence, or the variety of ways in which this influence was exercised. By the time of his death there were churches in Austria, Poland, Transylvania, and the Carpathians. In the Netherlands, Calvinism was replacing the Lutheran influence, and the first church was organized within Calvin's lifetime (1561). Here, as in Scotland, struggle against established authority aided the spread of a faith which was organized and disciplined so as to provide a good base for operations. As in Scotland and France, Calvinism became the inspiration for political as well as religious wars. By the time the Netherlands threw off the yoke of Spain (1609), Calvinism had become the established faith.

The impact of Geneva upon the world was not confined to Europe. New England bore testimony to a continued inspiration. Here, too, the basic ideas of a Calvinist Church were observed and transmitted to the New World. The appeal of Geneva cannot be confined to one nation or to one class of the population. In Scotland it first appealed to the powerful nobility, in France to the lesser nobility and the urban classes, in England to nobles, professional people, and middle-class elements. Many historians have regarded Calvinism as appealing especially to the middle classes because of Calvin's legalistic stand on usury, which all but destroyed the medieval limitations upon this practice. Others have seen this special appeal verified in the equation between worldly success and election which English preachers tended to make in the next century. Facts will not bear out such an interpretation, for the diversity of classes which accepted his faith remains to be explained. Many joined for reasons of salvation, for the sixteenth century was not yet a materialistic age; many others joined for political reasons, since Calvin, who abhorred revolt and maintained discipline in Geneva, founded a fighting faith which did not fear established authority and trembled only before the Lord.

A new Jerusalem had been created, and from it the impulse to create like centers of godliness swept over Europe. Ultimately, this momentum came from Geneva. It was Calvin who provided the dynamic element in Protestantism, and it seems only logical that the great clash between his faith and Catholicism was to dominate the history of Europe for nearly a century after his death.

CHAPTER . . . 4

The Middle Way

The English Reformation

Prelude to Reform. The English Reformation presents a special problem to the historian. It took over a century to define itself, and even then it did not do so completely. One historian has rightly called it a mood more than a system. The English Reformation was unique in that it settled on a broad middle road between Catholicism and Protestantism, and therefore deserves to be included among the attempts at reconciling the diverse forces which the Reformation unleashed.

F. M. Powicke has expressed this well: "The one definite thing that can be said about the Reformation in England is that it was an act of state." The king became the head of the Church and, with Parliament, legislated a new church organization, liturgy, and doctrine. This in itself was nothing new, for the princes, city councils, or kings of Lutheran Germany and Scandinavia had also imposed reform on the Church. But the English Reformation diverged from the European examples by failing to provide a complete theological basis for the church.

In England, as in Germany, the first decades of the sixteenth century were times of religious upheaval. Ever since the days of Wycliffe, isolated groups had continued to band together in order to study the Bible and to transmit theological views. Though these Lollards were scattered, their beliefs gave a significant turn to heresy and dissent in several important regions such as that of the diocese of York in the north. Denying the doctrines of transubstantiation, they opposed the nature of the Mass long before the Reformation. Moreover, Lollards were anticlerical, attacking both monks and priests. Pilgrimages and the use of images in churches were among the religious customs they deplored. This was a religious radicalism. It continued to exist in England side by side with the established Reformation. Though suppressed by the government, it nevertheless had some appeal, as a wide variety of heresy trials can attest.

For us the importance of Lollardy lies in the effect that the continental Reformation may have had upon this dissenting group. There seems to be little doubt that some Lollards were attracted to Lutheranism and that they formed the nucleus of that mysterious association of "Christian Brethren," who financed some of the early English Protestant literature, including Tyndale's translation of the Bible. But there were also other channels through which Lutheran ideas penetrated into England. The considerable trade between England and Germany afforded easy passage for Lutheran publications, and soon heresy permeated the merchant classes. In addition to this, the University of Cambridge began to harbor dissent. Here a small group of scholars known as "little Germany" met regularly to discuss the latest writings from the Reformation in that country.

This dissent, which after the advent of Luther tended

to become ever more heretical, attracted the attention of the authorities. It led to the ceremonial burning of Luther's tracts at Cambridge (1521), and to the trial of the German merchants of the Hanseatic League, who were accused of having smuggled Luther's writings into England. Members of the Cambridge group had to defend their views, but these trials produced recantations rather than martyrs (1527). Henry VIII entered the fray and wrote the book against Luther which brought him the title of "Defender of the Faith" from a grateful pope. It is difficult to evaluate the strength or persistence of Lutheranism in England. The fact remains that it does not seem to have greatly influenced the Reformation, and Robert Barnes of Cambridge emerges as the only English Lutheran of any significance.

Nevertheless, there existed doctrinal opposition to the Church, although it was never as significant as the anticlericalism of many elements of the population. In England, as on the Continent, there was widespread resistance to the Church's coercive jurisdiction and its monetary exactions. The prerogatives of the Church seemed arbitrary, and the religious returns pitifully small. With notable exceptions (for example, John Fisher), the English bishops were not outstanding clerics. Usually they were men of affairs, protégés of royal government, "experienced bureaucrats," as they have been called by one Catholic historian. They met the crisis of the Reformation by espousing the cause of the king. Most of the regular English clergy were untrained men whose lives were occupied with the care of their parishioners; no resistance to the king's policies could be expected from any clerical quarter.

The condition of the religious houses of the time has occasioned much controversy, for Thomas Cromwell's inspection of them for Henry VIII resulted in an indictment describing unspiritual living. But that inspection was designed to find grounds for an indictment and has to be taken with much caution. Here, as on the Continent, many houses carried on a life of

spiritual perfection, and many did not. However, there
was an excessive number of religious houses—eight hundred monasteries for a population of roughly three
million; one monastery for every ten parishes was over-
generous. This meant that examples of degenerate monastic life could be multiplied, while those equally
numerous ones which followed the accepted tradition
could be ignored. Moreover, before their dissolution
many monasteries had come under the economic man-
agement of neighboring gentry, and thus were eyed
by this important class as desirable spoils. Whatever
the state of the ecclesiastical hierarchy, priests were
not sufficiently popular for laymen to take up their
cause; many preferred royal dominance over the Church
to ecclesiastical tyranny.

These causes for discontent were brought to a head
by the rule of Cardinal Wolsey (1515–1529). His control
over the Church served as the immediate prelude to
the English Reformation. Wolsey's rise to power was
due to royal favor, and the good will of Henry VIII
was necessary before the cardinal could issue authoritative directives to Church or State. That this was the
case, even during the height of Wolsey's power, can be
seen from the speed of his fall once royal favor was
withdrawn. Nevertheless, the use to which Wolsey put
his position made him appear in the eyes of his contemporaries as the *de facto* ruler of England. Not only
did the cardinal dominate secular politics, but his
power extended to every part of the ecclesiastical hierarchy. Wolsey obtained the office of papal legate in
England, which meant that, within limits, he could
exercise the pope's powers in the area of his jurisdiction. In Wolsey, Church and State met; his power extended over both the spiritual and the temporal.

To many Englishmen this must have seemed a dramatic assertion of the power of the Church in England.
But there was another side to the picture. Wolsey's
example demonstrated to Henry VIII that Church and
State could be fused to form an engine of immense

power. Why should not the king, once he had relieved his deputy of all power, occupy the same position as Wolsey? Would not Henry show more concern for national interests than the cardinal, who could justly be accused of using his power to promote his own selfish ends? For Wolsey was interested in using his position to play a dominant role in European affairs. It was his aim to make England the arbiter of the balance of power on the Continent; thus he supported France against the overwhelming might of Charles V. By means of this foreign policy, the cardinal hoped to secure his election to the papacy, but the victories of Charles over France nullified Wolsey's schemes. His policy had not benefited England, had cost much in English money, and had alienated Charles V. After the sack of Rome by troops of the emperor (1527), the papacy was under the control of Charles, and he was hardly inclined to view any of Wolsey's schemes with favor. This, as much as the fact that Catherine of Aragon was his aunt, prejudiced Charles against Henry's divorce proceedings. Wolsey's foreign policy prepared the way for his downfall.

Wolsey was the protagonist of royal supremacy, though he would have been surprised at this estimate of his role in English history. The cardinal was not a man who lacked faith; indeed, he flirted with Christian Humanism and dissolved certain monastic establishments in order to endow colleges at Oxford and Ipswich. But of his unpopularity at the time of his fall there can be little doubt. His dictatorial temperament had dispensed with Parliament, which met only once during his fourteen years of power, and his use of the office of chancellor to settle cases speedily without referring to the common-law courts incited the animosity of judges and lawyers alike. Finally, his iron rule over the Church caused the clergy to resent him, and this was one important reason why churchmen showed so little resistance to the encroachments of the king upon papal power.

Wolsey's fall was the prelude to the subjugation of
the Church, which in turn was a result of the king's
divorce proceedings.

The King's Divorce. Why Henry VIII wanted to dis-
solve a happy marriage of eighteen years' standing
has long been a matter of dispute. It seems probable
that a variety of considerations led Henry to take this
step. He was in love with Anne Boleyn, and Ann's
ambitious relations wanted to see her become queen
in order that they might gain influence at court. A
more serious argument for divorce was Catherine's
failure to produce a male heir to the throne. The
dynastic Wars of the Roses, which had ended at Bos-
worth Field (1485), were not long past, and only one
woman, Matilda, daughter of Henry I, had previously
aspired to the throne. Her strife-ridden candidacy was
hardly an encouraging precedent for a female sovereign.
Thus, the fact that Catherine had borne the king a
daughter, Mary, did not settle the question of succession. The king's conscience must also be taken into
consideration. Catherine had been his brother's wife,
and the passage in Leviticus (XX, 21) seemed to Henry
like a judgment on heirless kings: "And if a man
shall take his brother's wife it is an unclean thing. . . .
They shall remain childless." Henry, as an amateur
theologian, must have viewed this divine judgment
with alarm.

Wolsey was not averse to the divorce; he disliked
Catherine, who was linked with Spain and with
Charles V by family ties and national sympathy. Indeed, Catherine jumped to the conclusion that Wolsey
was the instigator of the divorce action. Initially it
seemed as if all would be settled as the king wished,
for Wolsey, as legate, might get the pope's consent
to try the case in England so that he could give the
verdict in favor of divorce. This was an important
point, for all theologians agreed that only the pope

could judge whether the king had sinned by living with his brother's widow, or whether the original dispensation for Henry's marriage to Catherine was valid.

Wolsey's greatest mistake lay in the fact that he overplayed his hand with the pope from the beginning. His vanity and arrogance ruined his chances of becoming the sole judge of the divorce question. The cardinal, demanding absolute powers in the divorce action, told the pope that since he was legate in England, the integrity and conscience of the pope would come to no harm in his hands. Thus Wolsey arrogated to himself papal powers. Even the compromising, mild Clement VII could not allow this, especially since Charles V controlled Rome. A compromise was negotiated, and Cardinal Campeggio, who had already proven his skill in negotiations with the Lutherans, was delegated to try the case in England. No one knew of the pope's private instructions to Campeggio to use dilatory tactics and not to reach a decision until further orders. The result was that the trial proceeded (1529), but Campeggio adjourned the court for the summer without delivering a judgment. When it was due to convene again, the pope had recalled the suit to Rome. He did so in order to avoid a showdown, for Charles's power was now at its apex. The first act in the divorce question had resulted in an impasse. Henry was not inclined to accept the virtual destruction of his ambitions. The direct result of this stalemate was the removal of Wolsey; the long-range result was the beginning of the subjugation of the English Church.

That subjugation was begun by Henry after Wolsey's fall, partly to bring pressure to bear upon the pope, and partly to seize the opportunity for an assertion of royal control. In view of his efforts to preserve as much theological orthodoxy as possible, it is improbable that the king pursued a purposeful plan in his opposition to Rome, but rather Henry seems to have been driven by the pressure of events. Henry VIII was no reformer

of the Lutheran or Calvinist variety; his efforts were
always directed toward political control rather than
theological change.

Henry's first step was to use a legal weapon against
the clergy. Medieval statutes were reinterpreted to
justify action against the clergy for recognizing Wolsey's legatine authority. It was a singular piece of
impudence to accuse the clergy of obeying a man
whose tyranny they had deplored, but who was placed
over them because the king had willed it. Nevertheless,
the clergy had to pay a subsidy as fine, and had to
acknowledge Henry as "Protector and Supreme Head
of the English Church and Clergy" (1531). That same
year the king removed Catherine from court, thus clearly signifying his intentions.

Continued silence from Rome incited Henry to more
drastic action, now in cooperation with Parliament.
The use of Parliament in the subjugation of the
Church meant that Henry could claim the mandate
of his people for his antipapal legislation instead of
acting on his own initiative as an heretical monarch.
He seemed to be yielding to the will of his subjects.

The petition against the Ordinaries of the Realm
(1532) illustrates Henry's ingenius proceedings. The
petition was brought forward by the government, yet
it included enough real grievances against the clergy
to command parliamentary sponsorship and support.
It contained the request that the clergy should in future
make no canons (church laws) without royal approval.
Henry gracefully allowed the petition of his subjects
and thus gained a convenient weapon with which
to attack the legislative independence of the Church.
At the same time, the Act in Conditional Restraint
of Annates threatened to cut off a source of papal income—the first year's revenue from a bishopric. The
real intention of the act was clarified by the proviso
that its execution should depend upon the king's will.
Again Henry had obtained a weapon against the
pope to use as he saw fit.

The collaboration with Parliament provided Henry with threats to papal power which could aid in bringing the divorce proceedings at Rome to a successful conclusion. But Henry's bargaining powers, though strengthened, did not meet with success and time was pressing. Anne Boleyn was awaiting the birth of a child, a possible male heir to the throne (in reality the future Queen Elizabeth) and the divorce became a necessity in order to legitimize the prospective heir. At the instigation of the government, Parliament passed the Act in Restraint of Appeals (1533). This marks the climax in the subjugation of the Church. It eradicated the pope's jurisdiction in England and made the court of the archbishop of Canterbury the ecclesiastical court of last resort. Thus the English clergy, controlled by the king, could find its own interpretation of the faith and could enforce it in national ecclesiastical tribunals. This act made possible the state religion which was to form the basis of the English Reformation.

Parliament's action was followed by that of the new archbishop of Canterbury, Thomas Cranmer, who declared Henry's marriage to Catherine null and void. The inevitable reply from Rome followed swiftly; Clement declared Henry excommunicate (July 1533), and the king retaliated by putting the Act against Annates into operation. The break with Rome was complete, but this was only the beginning of the problems of the English Church. What was to be the fate of traditional church organization? Was the break with Rome to include also a break with Catholic dogma and liturgy? These were questions which were to haunt the English Church throughout its history, for the political break preceded any serious discussion of theological reform.

The Henrician Church. Once the break with Rome had been accomplished, the consolidation of the English Church went forward with some speed. Papal

revenues were cut off; the traditional payment of
"Peter's pence" ceased (1534). In the same year any
papal share in the appointment of bishops was abolished and a new Heresy Act was passed, which typically
enough lacked definition, but which gave the state
the initiative in persecution. The climax was reached in
November with the enactment of the Act of Supremacy
which confirmed the king's right to be "taken, accepted, and reputed the only supreme head on earth
of the Church in England." This act transferred to
the king the pope's administrative rights in England,
including the right of visitation and reformation of
ecclesiastical bodies.

The wealth and partial corruption of the monastic
system made it a convenient target for the king's newly
won power. Evidence was gathered by the crown
through visitations of monasteries and convents by
Thomas Cromwell; this evidence provided the opportunity for parliamentary action. First, the minor
monastic establishments were dissolved (1536), and then,
three years later, the more venerable houses which
had survived the earlier purge (1539). Henry failed to
use the income gained through dissolution to support
charitable causes. Instead, he used his plunder to pay
off his creditors and to finance his foreign and domestic
policies. But with this he combined a shrewd effort
to gain support for his reformation. The monastic lands
were sold at low prices to neighboring gentry. This
influential class became the loyal supporters of the
Tudors and of their policies. They now had a stake in
royal supremacy and they formed a barrier against
the restoration of a religious system which might de-
prive them of their economic gains.

Nevertheless, the dissolution of the monasteries incited the only mass protest against the crown. The
partisans of the Pilgrimage of Grace (1536) demanded
a return to the traditional order of things and an end
to such radical policies as dissolution. The bulk of the

"pilgrims" came from the North, from the counties bordering Scotland, which had a tradition of border warfare and political semi-independence. Economic distress and resistance to any interference in their traditional mode of life combined to make these border peoples a constant source of trouble. Queen Elizabeth was to experience the same difficulties with the North but, like her father, she too was able to cope successfully with such a threat (that is, the rising of the northern earls, 1569).

The Pilgrimage of Grace was the only popular uprising, but there were individual protests which focused attention on the fundamental issues of Henry's Reformation. Thomas More was no active revolutionary. Indeed, he had succeeded Wolsey as chancellor and throughout the early stages of the divorce proceedings had maintained silence on the king's great problem. For More was attached to Henry by bonds of friendship and mutual respect. He had helped the king to write his book against Luther, and in turn Henry had patronized More, the Humanist friend of Colet and Erasmus. As a Christian Humanist, More had been critical of many aspects of church organization. In his *Utopia*, he sketched a society based on reason and co-operation. Nevertheless, as soon as the Lutheran menace to the Church became apparent, More had rallied to orthodoxy and had been instrumental in the persecution of heretics. For him, revolt was not the solution, for he believed in the divine sanction of the church's organization. Like many of his fellow Humanists, he was not opposed to the medieval tradition itself. More's conservatism, strengthened by his legal training and experience, led him to believe strongly in permanent laws, chief of which was the law of God. Against it, no human law could stand. This was the common legal theory of the time, but for More it had added significance, for church organization was included in the commands of the law of God. It was over this point

that he broke with Henry: he was unable to eliminate
the pope from the Church and substitute the headship of the king. This meant tyranny, not Christian
rule.

More's execution (1535) was the price he paid for
his convictions. John Fisher, bishop of Rochester, followed him to the Tower and to execution, while
Reginald Pole, a close relative of the king, went into
exile. Such resistance was rare. A whole group of men
also reared in the Humanist tradition adjusted their
thinking to the king's wishes. They also took their
stand on traditional theories. Nonresistance to royal
authority was their motto; sedition and rebellion were
dangerous to the state, and besides, kings were instituted by God. Did not David refuse to kill King Saul
despite the wrongs done to him? But these writers did
not make the king absolute. In the tradition of Christian Humanism they emphasized the king's moral re-
sponsibilities toward his subjects.

Yet there were others who seem to have worked
toward royal absolutism in this crisis. Thomas Cromwell symbolized the type of royal servant for whom
the king's wish was law. Cromwell was Henry's main
instrument for translating his ideas into practical action.
He has been accused of following Machiavelli's ideas,
but the only evidence that he ever read *The Prince*
comes from his avowed enemy, Reginald Pole. Cromwell was no theorist, but a practical civil servant of
the type prominent in the new western monarchies.

His fall from power was not linked with theoretical
considerations, but with court intrigues and failure
to execute royal policy successfully. Cromwell's chief
enemy at court was Stephen Gardiner, who within a
decade was to switch from being one of the most
extreme proponents of royal supremacy to submission
to Catholicism. Gardiner typifies best one other important aspect of the English Reformation; his theological position never varied. Like his royal master, he

wanted Catholic dogma without a pope. He was the most powerful opponent of Protestantism at court, and consequently he spent part of Edward VI's reign in prison, protesting against England's drift towards Protestant radicalism. Thus, it was not difficult for Gardiner to submit to the pope upon the accession of Queen Mary.

It was Gardiner's opposition to Protestantism which gave him a lever against Thomas Cromwell, for Cromwell believed that England could not isolate herself from the Protestant-Catholic alignment in Europe, and attempted to negotiate an alliance with the German Lutheran princes. Henry at first lent his reluctant support and Robert Barnes served as negotiator. Yet the king never intended the reformation of the Church along Lutheran lines, while the German princes made the introduction of Lutheranism into England the prerequisite for an alliance with a monarch whom they did not trust. Only the shrewd Philip of Hesse was willing to put political agreement first and theological concord second. Henry broke off the negotiations as soon as it became clear that Charles V's military preparations were directed against the Turk rather than against England. Thus, it was not the urgliness of Anne of Cleves, whom the king was to marry in order to cement the alliance, which ruined the projected pact. Cromwell's enemies, led by Gardiner, seized this opportunity to bring about the downfall of the chief advocate of the Lutheran alliance. They were successful. Thomas Cromwell's execution (1540) was followed by that of Robert Barnes.

The deaths of Cromwell and Barnes meant the failure of a rapprochement with Lutheranism. What then was the theological basis of the English Church? The Six Articles (1539) show the reaction against Protestant entanglements. They tended to reaffirm the Catholic doctrine of the sacraments, the confessional, the mass, and the celibacy of the clergy. Yet these articles were not quite as severe as they first appeared. Their phrasing was ambiguous on such matters as the sacraments, and they expressed disapproval of saints, images, and certain ceremonies. This was due in large measure to Thomas Cranmer, the archbishop of Canterbury.

Thomas Cranmer had left Cambridge in order to aid the king with his divorce. He had organized the collection of opinions from European universities about the legality of the king's marriage, and Henry had recognized his ability by appointing him to the key post of archbishop of Canterbury (1532). Cranmer was an academician and a theologian; his ideas went much further in the direction of Protestantism than Henry was willing to go. Cranmer kept in constant touch with the European reformers and he regarded the English Church not as a national church, but as a part of the common body of Christendom which was attempting to purify itself. Thus he asked Melanchthon, without success, to write the English prayer book. It was Cranmer who constantly sought Bullinger's advice, and who invited Bucer to spend his declining years in England. Henry was aware of Cranmer's bias toward international Protestantism, but he continued to use him and to trust him. Thomas Parker's explanation for this seems convincing: from Henry's point of view it was not a bad thing to have an archbishop more radical than himself; he would not have to drive a reluctant partner, but merely restrain one who was too eager. It should be added that Cranmer was a moderate Protestant, and in many ways a compromiser in the tradition of Melanchthon. He favored latitudinarianism in the church, and his lack of doctrinaire views, together with his belief in royal supremacy, made him hesitate, when Mary restored Catholicism, before deciding that no compromise was possible.

A hesitant theological policy thus accompanied the political consolidation of royal supremacy. Ultimately, the Henrician Reformation was to have greater political than religious consequences for England. It meant an increase in royal power; Henry no longer regarded the maintenance of peace as his primary function, but he now claimed to be the preserver of the unity of church and people. In the name of such unity, many individual rights could be destroyed. However, enhancement of royal supremacy was not the immediate result of the Henrician Reformation, but instead, an increase in the power of the king working with Parliament, for the religious change had been accomplished with and through Parliament.

This had a great significance for England's future, for elsewhere in Europe parliaments were going out of fashion. Before the Reformation, Parliament had only been convoked occasionally, and since the accession of the Tudors, even more seldom. The Reformation Parliament spanned seven years, although not in continuous session. In that length of time it was able to develop procedures and start a journal. It had helped make the Reformation, and from now on could claim that any ecclesiastical change had to be approved by the two houses. Nor was Parliament as servile to the king as has been alleged. Thomas Cromwell was bitter about the resistance which he encountered, and Henry's cherished Statute of Proclamations (1539) was considerably amended by Parliament. The statute as projected would have given the force of law to all the king's proclamations, but the only way in which it could pass Parliament was to recognize solely such royal proclamations as did not conflict with acts of Parliament, the law of the land, or the property rights of the subjects. Perhaps the greatest achievement of Henry's Reformation was that it helped preserve parliamentary power in England at a time when royal absolutism was becoming the rule in Europe. This was scarcely Henry's intention; the consolidation of parliamentary power would have displeased him no less than the theological changes which transpired after his death.

Protestant Revolt and Catholic Reaction. The short
reign of Edward VI witnessed revolution in liturgy and
dogma. Edward was only nine years old when his father
died, and it was his uncle, Edward Seymour, duke of
Somerset, who became regent protector of England.
Somerset was a convinced Protestant, but cautious and
moderate in his attitude toward religious change. While
he did not want to repress those who believed in
religious innovations (the Act of the Six Articles, as
well as the statutes against heresy, was repealed), yet he
wanted uniformity imposed to safeguard public order.
The Act of Uniformity (1549) defined conformity for
the whole realm according to the First Prayer Book
of Edward VI. It was the first prayer book in the
English tongue, displacing the service books of the
Middle Ages. As a guide to ecclesiastical practice, the
book was an exercise in ambiguity. Despite its conservatism on vestments and the mass, Protestants could use
the service with good conscience. On many important
theological points the book preserved significant silence.

The First Prayer Book of Edward VI established a
pattern which was to transcend the short life of the
book itself and become a fundamental mode of procedure in the English Church. What occurred was the
passage by Parliament of a succession of Acts of Uniformity which provided for conformity to the various
prayer books. The content of these books was broad
enough to allow for a large degree of latitudinarianism
within the national church. For the Tudors, political
allegiance was always of greater importance than theological definition, and Somerset followed this pattern.
It was after his fall from power that England seemed
to join the mainstream of the Protestant revolt.

Somerset's fall was due to court intrigue which was
aided by the economic unrest resulting from the en-
closure movement. Rising prices increased the economic
dilemma of the small man, and the result was Kett's
rebellion (1549). The uprising in Norfolk was not concerned with religion but with economics; indeed, the

rebels were Protestant in sentiment. Somerset was sympathetic to their cause, and this gave his rival, the earl of Warwick (later duke of Northumberland), his opportunity to seize power.

Northumberland was Protestant mainly because of his desire to despoil church properties. Somerset had already dissolved the chantries, those pious foundations which provided the money for the celebration of masses for the dead. The proceeds of the dissolution were to be used for educational and charitable purposes, and some of the wealth was used to found grammar schools which bear the name of King Edward VI. Northumberland seized church plate in order to pay the king's debts and to enrich himself. The duke's selfish reasons for being a Protestant meant that he took little interest in theological questions, and this left the field open for Cranmer to act with an authority which he had not enjoyed before this time.

For all his moderation, Cranmer was becoming increasingly convinced that Zwinglian Protestantism might have theological validity. The Second Act of Uniformity enjoined allegiance to the Second Prayer Book of Edward VI (1552). This prayer book emphasized Protestant ideas and introduced a much more austere service; vestments were abolished and the altar became merely a communion table. English usage now paralleled Zwinglian liturgy, and it is significant that Bucer's more conservative suggestions were rejected. Moreover, this liturgical reform affected all the laity, for the Second Act of Uniformity compelled the attendance of all Englishmen at religious services, an example Queen Elizabeth was to follow.

The success of this shift toward a more definite Protestant theology depended not on popular support, but upon the good will of those in power. Northumberland was willing to give his support. However, he was not king, but regent, and thus the fragile and sick young monarch was the pillar upon whom this reform had to depend. The next heir was Mary, and she had refused to follow the Acts of Uniformity; like her mother, Catherine of Aragon, she was a pious Catholic. Edward's death precipitated a crisis. Northumberland's attempted substitution of the Protestant Lady Jane Grey failed, and Mary became queen (1553).

History has not been kind to Mary; the fires of Smithfield and her eventual failure in all she undertook have made her one of the most maligned of English sovereigns. Yet Mary's main weakness was that she was the only really pious Tudor. She was obsessed with the idea of restoring the traditional faith at any price, to save her subjects' souls and her own. But she moved slowly at the beginning of her reign, counselled and aided by Cardinal Reginald Pole, who was moderate rather than fanatic. Could the clock be successfully turned back? The Act of Repeal (1553), which was supposed to undo the Reformation, revealed clearly that there was to be no unconditional surrender to the pope. Papal bulls were given legal force, but only if they did not conflict with English laws and royal dignity. Moreover, before getting any action, Pole had to sanction the possession of the church lands by those who had acquired them during the Reformation; there was to be no economic restitution. In order to make sure that its feelings on this point did not go unnoticed, Parliament passed a bill confirming abbey lands to their possessors. Indeed, Mary had to face constant parliamentary reluctance. Parliament was getting valuable training in opposing government measures. Mary had at least this in common with her father: both, against their will, furthered the growth of Parliament as a powerful institution in the realm.

Mary's two great mistakes were marriage with Philip of Spain and the increasing persecution of heretics. The unpopular marriage linked Catholicism and Spain in the popular mind. The sacrifice of national independence for allegiance to the powerful center of the Counter Reformation seemed to be the consequence of

Catholic restoration. This was to be the severest handicap Catholicism had to face in England. What the marriage between Mary and Philip had begun, the Armada was to complete. Henceforth, the national church became identified with national independence. The persecutions for heresy also gave Protestantism the popular support it had lacked during the reign of Edward. Those burned at Smithfield were not only mighty men like Cranmer, but humble folk who had the sympathy of their equals. John Foxe's *Book of Martyrs* (1563) made sure that these men were not forgotten and gave to English Protestantism its chronicle of martyrs for the faith.

Mary did return England to papal allegiance but never wholly so, and only at the price of strengthening Protestant sympathies within England. But it can be argued that the most important development for the future took place among those Englishmen who were in voluntary exile during Mary's reign. These men went to Geneva or to the Rhineland and there came into close touch with continental Protestant movements. Leaders who were determined to build a new Jerusalem in England, and who could not be coerced by political considerations from the path of theological righteousness, returned from the Swiss cantons or from Germany after Mary's death. John Ponet and Christopher Goodman exalted the law of God above monarchs, and for them the supremacy of God and the true faith was independent of royal supremacy. Thus Mary's reign prepared the way for the Puritan challenge to the English Church.

Mary's death (1558) did not close the age of the Reformation in England, but instead brought to the fore new problems. Her half-sister and successor, Elizabeth, faced not only the struggle between royal supremacy and Catholicism, but a defense of the national church against attacks by both Protestants and Catholics.

The Elizabethan Settlement. It was not obvious upon Elizabeth's accession to the throne what her ecclesiastical policy would be. This was typical of the new queen's methods of procedure. She revealed her position only when necessary, and attempted to satisfy as many of her subjects as possible in order to achieve unity. The Elizabethan Settlement was built upon national unity and not upon theological considerations. The queen may be classed as a "politique," whose guiding principle was the preservation of her power and the unity of the nation. She chose a middle road, endeavoring to make the national church as inclusive as possible, thus creating an instrument for national unity rather than for denominational dissension.

The success of her mode of action is evidenced by the fact that the pope did not excommunicate her until twelve years after her accession (1570), and that Philip of Spain did not proceed by force against England until thirty years had elapsed (1588). Elizabeth was a realist in politics, but not the only one on the European scene in the second half of the sixteenth century. The religious wars which the Reformation had caused made the preservation of royal power the prime concern of most of her fellow monarchs. But Elizabeth, in contrast to many of these rulers, never buttressed monarchical power with a theory of the Divine Right of Kings; she was not given to excessive theorizing. Pragmatism was the characteristic feature of her secular and ecclesiastical policies.

The first prayer book of her reign reflected her methodology (1559). It was essentially the second prayer book of her brother's reign, with alterations which made it more palatable to Catholic opinion. By the substitution of vague phrases for well defined doctrine, both Protestants and Catholics could be satisfied. The new Supremacy Act substituted "Supreme Governor" for "Supreme Head," in order to make the title less offensive. The Act of Uniformity enforced allegiance to the new liturgy. Elizabeth was concerned about her control over the church, for the matter of ecclesiastical discipline involved royal power. Clerical visitations were once again annexed to the powers of the crown, and the Court of High Commission enforced allegiance to her church policies. Nor did she abolish bishops as the Protestants wished. This was not merely because she wished to introduce reform gradually, but because she could use bishops as disciplinary instruments. On this point she refused to compromise, and those who opposed her were, so the queen thought, attacking her royal power and sowing national disunity.

For the men who had come home from exile with ambitions of establishing a more thorough Protestantism in England, the queen's policy was a bitter disappointment. To them it was "cloaked papistry." Ambiguity in the definition of theological points was unacceptable to men who had watched the European Reformation in action. Elizabeth was now confronted with opposition from the Protestant side from within the church itself, for most of these reformers did not openly secede from the Anglican Church. They began by attacking the wearing of clerical vestments as "popish" customs (circa 1564–1567). Elizabeth managed to weather that storm, but growing sympathy for more extreme Protestantism on the part of Parliament gave cause for alarm.

Elizabeth attempted to defend the ecclesiastical establishments from parliamentary interference, but the ambiguity in the implementation of the Reformation created new problems. The king, with Parliament, had legislated the changes of the Reformation. Did that mean that the monarch alone had the right to initiate such legislation? That is what had happened in the past, but now Parliament asserted its leadership in ecclesiastical matters. The case of Strickland was typical. He had introduced a motion in the House of Commons for the reform of the Book of Common Prayer (1561). Elizabeth called him before her council and forbade him to take his seat in Parliament. This caused a furor in the House of Commons, and a compromise was arranged. Strickland could take his seat, but his motion was to be dropped.

It was by such compromises that the queen attempted to check a Parliament bent on establishing a religious policy of its own. But such compromises were two-edged swords. They preserved a semblance of unity, but they also strengthened the opposition through indirect concessions. And Parliament was receptive to the more extreme Protestant ideas of the "Puritan party."

This party was not a cohesive body of men, nor did it have a well defined theology. The Puritans agreed on the need for a simpler and more Protestant form of church organization, and thus were opposed to bishops as well as to vestments. They also had in common the idea of the overriding power of God and the necessity of Scripture. Only after the middle of Elizabeth's reign did Calvinistic influences assert themselves. Thomas Cartwright became the leader of the Presbyterian wing of the Puritans. Under his influence an admonition was drawn up and presented to Parliament, urging the establishment of a Presbyterian discipline as the substitute for Episcopacy (1572).

The Puritans' main weapon against the church was preaching or "prophesying." This was preaching by laymen not licensed by the church. These preachers used a simple scriptural approach in their sermons, which contrasted with the learning sometimes exhibited by the Anglican clerics. They had great popular appeal; therefore, the government did its best to suppress such practices. Indeed the Puritans have been defined as a preaching order; such a definition takes into account the great varieties of Puritan religious expression, from Cartwright's Presbyterianism to the radicalism of the followers of Robert Brown, who believed in the self-sufficiency and independence of each congregation.

Elizabeth tried to minimize this opposition as much as possible. A stricter Act of Uniformity (1571) did drive some of the Puritanically inclined clergy from their livings, but it was not until the 1580s that the government decided to follow a sterner course. Elizabeth's first archbishop of Canterbury, Matthew Parker, had been a man of great moderation, who supported the queen's policy of a broad and inclusive church, and who was loath to resort to any kind of persecution. Moreover, his successor, Archbishop Grindal, had sympathized with Puritan views and the queen was forced to dismiss him from office. It was Grindal's successor, Archbishop Whitgift (1583–1604), who began a more active policy against Puritanism. Cartwright was deprived of his Cambridge fellowship, and Whitgift, as the defender of Anglicanism, personally entered the pamphlet warfare to which the Puritans had resorted against the church. The Marprelate Tracts (1588–1589), with their acrimonious attacks against bishops, climaxed Puritan agitation.

Elizabeth's reign did not end with a victory over Puritan dissent. Even the more forceful policy of the government had not meant that the issue was squarely joined. Only after James I called his conference at Hampton Court (1604) were the Puritans expelled from the Church of England, and even thereafter it was sometimes difficult to distinguish a Puritan from an Anglican. This was due both to the "broadness" of Anglicanism as well as to the fact that the Puritan party had no unified theology except in its Presbyterian wing. Nevertheless, the Puritan attack upon the church was a most dangerous portent for the future. Not only did the divines gather much popular support by their preaching, but a restive Parliament became increasingly willing to listen to Puritan ideas. Parliament could thereby assert its right to determine ecclesiastical policy.

Catholic opposition to Elizabeth's policies expressed itself on the domestic scene through missionary activity by priests trained at the newly established English Catholic College of Douai (1562). Plots against the queen's life in favor of Mary, Queen of Scots, Catholic candidate to the throne of England, were the political expressions of Catholic opposition. The danger of these activities was increased by their association with foreign policy. Philip of Spain attempted to destroy Elizabeth in order to restore England to Catholicism and to recover his formerly decisive influence over the island's foreign policy. This situation forced Elizabeth to act in a manner quite out of character with her policy of compromise. The execution of Mary, Queen of Scots, who had fled to England from the wrath of John Knox, became a political necessity (1587). As long as Mary lived, the queen was in mortal danger. But that execution brought on the war with Spain which Elizabeth had endeavored to avoid. Philip was now certain that conquest was the only way to bring England into the Catholic camp. The defeat of the Armada (1588) did not end the war, but it did assure England freedom from invasion, and Elizabeth continued to harass Philip by aiding his rebellious Dutch subjects. The war with Spain completely identified Catholicism with the national enemy. It no longer constituted a serious internal threat, though it survived in the more remote regions of the northern counties. Elizabeth had defeated Catholicism in England, even if she had not dealt effectively with the Puritan Protestant threat to the organization of her church.

The evidence tends to show that both Catholics and Puritans were minorities in England and that, by the time the aged queen died, the majority of her subjects were content to worship in the national church. The theological *via media* which even permitted Puritanically inclined ministers within the church suited the temper of the population.

The Elizabethan Settlement was not without theoretical defenders. At Whitgift's request, Richard Hooker defended the Elizabethan Church on grounds which had nothing to do with expediency. Hooker based his defense of Anglicanism upon the exaltation of human reason. Every man was born with the light of reason, and could therefore discern the "good." That good was determined through the universal law of nature in which the scriptures participated. Thus Hooker attacked the Puritans' sole reliance upon the Scriptures. The Anglican Church had been established by a Parliament representing the whole realm. Surely a whole nation could not lack that divine reason with which every man was born. Harmony was all important to Hooker and one of the cardinal precepts of the law of nature. Puritans in attacking the Anglican settlement were destroying a God-given harmony and contravening the combined "reason" of the nation. Law and harmony: these were the key concepts which Hooker utilized to justify the Anglican settlement, and both were instituted by God and both expressed man's reason.

Hooker's *Laws of Ecclesiastical Policy* (circa 1594–1597) reflected Elizabeth's approach to the government of her realm, though she could not have relished Hooker's strong conviction that kings also should be bound by law, or his emphasis on the part of Parliament in the making of the English Reformation.

Attempts at Reconciliation

Protestant and Catholic. The Church of England had provided an inclusive Protestantism. Could the various branches of Christendom which the Reformation had called to life find unity on the basis of a common core of belief? There were men who thought that this could be accomplished. Their efforts were directed toward finding a basis for agreement between Protestants and Catholics, as well as among Protestants themselves. That these efforts were doomed to failure does not make them less interesting or significant. What was the reaction of the Catholic Church to the Reformation, and what attempts were made to reconcile these two branches of Christendom?

Leo X had tried to combat schism by bribing the rulers of Europe with concessions in church appoint-

ments and finance. He did succeed in the case of
France, where a Concordat (1516) gave the king the
right to appoint clerical officers, the pope retaining
merely a veto power. This arrangement was a vital
factor in Francis I's later opposition to reform. But
such political maneuvering alone could not overcome
the Reformation; a religious revival was needed to re-
establish contact between the Church and the pious
masses of the population. Such a revival had already
begun by the time Luther posted his theses about indulgences. Not only had laymen established such reform organizations as the Brethren of the Common
Life, but the regular clergy had begun to renew their
religious fervor. The tentative efforts at reconciliation
with Protestants originated with the clergy, for the
unity of all believers in Christ was an essential part
of their religious thought.

The most important agency in these efforts was the
Oratory of Divine Love in Rome (circa 1517). This
was a small but powerful body, which included in its
membership many dignitaries of the Church. Its members believed that the best way to spread reform was
by example; hence, they practiced prayer, frequent
confession, communion, and charity. The clerics of
the oratory formed a contemplative rather than a
militant group, related by temper and outlook to
Christian Humanism. Such men were well fitted to
mediate between Catholicism and Protestant reform
movements.

Two of the oratory's members were to play a leading part in the negotiations with the Protestants:
Cardinal Gaspard Contarini and Cardinal Reginald
Pole. They believed in emphasizing the Scriptures
rather than the traditions of the Church, in simplifying
religious services, and in salvation through the certainty
of faith in Christ. Despite their Protestant tendencies,
they never clearly expounded these vital points, and
Pole advised a friend to believe that she could only
be saved by faith, but to act as if she could only

Pope Leo X. (*Three Lions*)

be saved by works. Nor did Pole or Contarini reject freedom of will; in this they followed Erasmus rather than Luther. Nevertheless, they were far removed from the spirit of the Renaissance papacy. Events conspired to aid their cause. The sack of Rome by the mercenary troops of Charles V, many of whom were infected with Lutheranism, meant the end of the Renaissance spirit in that city and in the papacy (1527). The terrible destruction and looting by the soldiers seemed like a judgment from God. To the Germans the looting of Rome was the culmination of all the prophecies of doom which had been made about "sinful" Rome throughout the centuries. It seemed the fulfillment of Ulrich von Hutten's cry: let the pope be overthrown and the usurpations of Rome returned to the German Reich. Looting and murder were accompanied by blasphemy as Spanish troops joined those from Germany. No wonder Clement VII believed that the dreadful prophecies of the book of the Apocalypse were about to come true, that the end of the world was at hand. Shortly before his death he asked Michelangelo to paint the last judgment on the ceiling of the Sistine Chapel. But what seemed like a prelude to the end of an epoch was in reality the dawn of a new beginning, for indeed, we can date the advent of the Catholic Reformation from the time of the sack of Rome. Contarini hailed Pope Paul III (1534–1549) for transforming Renaissance Rome into a model for Christendom. Paul III gave tentative support to the men of the Oratory and they now began their efforts at conciliation. Among the Protestants they found men willing to work to restore Christian unity. Both Bucer and Melanchthon were eager for compromise, especially since Pole and Contarini had decided that the Confession of Augsburg need not stand in the way of agreement.

The Colloquy of Regensburg (1541) was called to fulfill these hopes. At first real progress was made on the question of justification by faith; a compromise was

proposed which said nothing about either freedom of
the will or about the subjective certainty of justification. Melanchthon accepted this formulation of the
basic Protestant idea. Even Luther's old adversary,
Johannes Eck, agreed to this interpretation of justification by faith. But concord was short-lived. Differences
on the mass, on saints and papal supremacy could not
be reconciled. Luther was suspicious of the meeting,
and the Protestant princes failed to support it. Too
many vested interests were thriving on disunion, and
the gulf between Protestant and Catholic opinion could
no longer be bridged even by these men of good will.
Despite Bucer's efforts to restore harmony, a second
meeting at Regensburg (1546) failed even more dis-
mally.

This failure strengthened those in the Catholic
Church who had always been suspicious of the Regensburg venture. This faction was led by John Peter
Caraffa (later Pope Paul IV), who had also been a
member of the Oratory of Divine Love. Caraffa's
scheme for reform was not based on mediation but
rather upon the spiritual revival which the Spanish
Church had been experiencing ever since the beginning of the century. This revival stressed austerity and
religious discipline within the framework of orthodoxy.
The return of the monastic orders to the strictness
and devotion enjoined in their original charters had
initiated a reform movement which spread throughout
the Spanish Church. The Dominicans led the way; new
orders were founded and old orders reformed in Italy
as well as in Spain. These reforms included the purging
of all heretical elements. With the failure of Pole and
Contarini, Catholic reform followed this pattern.

Paul III was at first torn between the two approaches
to reform, but his inclination toward Caraffa's point
of view was shown in his renewal of the Inquisition
(1542). The aggressive spread of Calvinism furthered
the tightening of orthodoxy. Two prominent churchmen, Peter Martyr and Bernard of Occhino, went over

to Calvin (1542). Both were Italians, both were friends of Cardinal Pole, and Occhino was the general of the Capuchins. This further discredited the moderate Catholic party and provided excellent propaganda for those who wanted open war against heresy.

The Jesuit order had already been recognized by the pope (1540), and thus the chief offensive weapon of the papacy was ready for use. Like Calvin, Ignatius of Loyola was a believer in discipline, organization, and the preservation of a common and well-defined faith. His spiritual exercises disciplined the wills of his followers in order to make them obedient soldiers, ready to fight for the glory of the Church. To a Jesuit missionary like Edmund Campion the voice of the general of the order was "a warrant from heaven and oracle of Christ." His words reflect a fervor in the cause of the Church which rivalled the devotion of Calvin's followers: "The expense is reckoned, the enterprise is begun; it is of God, it cannot be withstood. So the faith was planted, so it must be restored." Here was an organization well fitted to fight Calvinism, and it was Geneva which constituted the most direct menace to the Church. Calvin had been present at Regensburg, but he had been less willing to compromise than his fellow reformers.

Nevertheless, there still remained one hope for reconciliation. In response to the pressure from Emperor Charles V, the pope had consented to the calling of a council of all Christendom in order to settle the schism. After much delay, this council met in the city of Trent (1545). Once more high hopes for reconciliation had to be abandoned, for the Protestants, after putting in a brief appearance, refused to continue attending a council guided by the pope.

The Council of Trent did not reunify Christendom, but instead reformulated and tightened Catholic dogma. This was a pressing necessity, for had not Catholics themselves ignored the papal bull excommunicating Luther and negotiated with the heretics? The real work of the council was done during the third session (1562–1563), when the Jesuits were instrumental in guiding the proceedings. What emerged was Catholic dogma well defined and authoritative. The council took a stand squarely opposed to Protestant theology; belief in justification by faith alone, belief in the primacy of Scripture over church tradition, and the denial of papal headship were branded as heretical. Church reform was attempted at last; simony, traffic in indulgences and abuses in monasticism were condemned. If these reforms had come a century before, the unity of Latin Christendom might have been preserved.

Reconciliation between Catholics and Protestants had proved impossible; the religious differences which had evolved during the two decades before the Colloquy of Regensburg could no longer be settled at the conference table. A century after the Council of Trent, the learned Bishop Bossuet told the Protestants, "Mutas? Ergo erras." [Do you introduce changes and innovations? Then you are in error.]

The Growing Differentiation. The differences between Protestantism and Catholicism did not remain confined to theology alone, they came to encompass divergent attitudes to the whole texture of religious experience and, through this, toward life itself. Catholicism now turned increasingly to that outward symbolizing of the might, power, and truth of the Church which Protestants had deplored from the beginning. A delight in grandiose religious ceremony, in liturgical color and form increasingly contrasted with Protestant simplicity. The trends in popular piety discussed earlier were reinvigorated. For some, Luther dispersed the clouds of foreboding under which so many of the common people lived; he had solved the problem of the awesome power of God and the helplessness of man. But for many others the mystical elements of a divine revelation continued closer to their spiritual needs. Pictorial representations of the miracles performed by saints began to be common, especially in Catholic Germany. The miracle became central to popular piety as well as that adoration of the Virgin Mary, which the Protestants constantly attacked.

The decrees of the Council of Trent on these matters had, therefore, a basis in the longings of popular piety itself; the dramatic in this piety was once more recaptured by the Church. Protestant regions experienced severe difficulties in restraining their peasants and villagers from crossing over into Catholic territories in order to participate in religious festivities. This popular piety was strongest in remote, tradition-oriented, rural areas, and it is small wonder that there Protestantism had gained little success from the very beginning. Yet this atmosphere permeated most of the Catholic world within half a century. The Jesuits pioneered in its diffusion. Their church in Rome, built toward the end of the century, concretized the dramatic urge of Catholicism's revitalized piety: it combined great theatrical vistas and use of light with a love of color centered around both the altar where the supreme miracle of the Mass was performed and the pulpit from which they inaugurated a renaissance of dynamic preaching. The church foreshadowed that *Roma Triumphans* of the next century which is the Rome of today: a capital thought fit to house the confident might and aspirations of the papacy.

In this manner a Catholic culture grew up which was quite different from that which Protestantism had advocated. But another fact must be added to illustrate the growing schism among the faiths. Differences in moral attitudes were to be important beyond their theological foundations. For Calvinists in particular, true morality was exemplified in the never-ending struggle between the world and the flesh. There could be no compromise between man plagued by the "old Adam" within himself and the utter perfection of God which served as a constant command and reminder. Catholicism, believing in free will, took a different attitude toward man. To be sure he was a fallen creature, but this meant that he might sometimes err and might, if the error was not mortal, gain absolution. For the end object was to train man's will to follow the good as best it could and not to expect humanity to live in constant battle. Just as the drama of the churches and the liturgy would aid fallible man by appealing to his instincts, so the same practicality determined the Catholic view of sin. Man, being what he is, needs such aids just as he needs an infallible authority, the divine church, to govern his spiritual life. This was quite a different view of man than that of Calvin's in which man, "naked but for his conscience," battles for righteousness in the "theatre of the world."

Two different views on the nature and capabilities of man confronted each other. As each of them permeated its geographic domain, the style of life of the inhabitants was deeply affected. The differences between the North and South of Europe, between, for example, the Netherlands and Italy, are not so much due to different climates but to the fact that Calvinist attitudes influence one region and not the other. People in Italy do not necessarily work less than those of the European north, but their attitude toward that work is of a different and lighter texture. The love for color and the greater zest for uninhibited self-expression in the South is not due merely to the sun and blue skies, which would not cover much of France in any case, but to the deep differences between Catholic and Protestant attitudes toward life. Thus, the Reformation had consequences which far exceed any theological quarrels; it led to a division which was one of cultural attitudes, indeed attitudes toward life itself. Reconciliation had failed at Regensburg, and while the rest of the sixteenth century witnessed attempts to resolve religious differences by force of arms, the two Europes which the Reformation had created were growing ever further apart. It took several centuries for them to draw closer together again, though the differences just explained were to remain alive into our own times.

Protestant Unity. If Catholics and Protestants could not achieve theological agreement, what about the multitudinous forms of Protestantism? Protestant disunity was apparent almost from the beginning of the Reformation. Luther had acquired fellow travelers with their own views and beliefs as soon as he had broken with the Church, and the reformers of the second generation in their turn differed from Lutheranism. Yet, strenuous efforts (though generally resulting in failure) were made for unity among the reformers; Martin Bucer initiated many of these conferences, attempting to evolve formulas of concord around which the reformers could unite.

For Bucer, the fiasco at Marburg was but the beginning of increased efforts of mediation. The climax came at the Wittenberg Conference (1536); there Bucer agreed to modify his own beliefs in order to achieve an understanding with Luther. In the Wittenberg Concord he subscribed to the main articles of the Augsburg Confession. This was not a compromise but a unilateral agreement between the Strassburg reformer and Luther. For Luther, compromise was not the way to concord; only the retraction of false beliefs could result in agreement. Bucer's hope that the Wittenberg Concord would also be signed by the Swiss was never realized. Bullinger refused to adopt a Lutheran point of view.

Bucer's supposition that there was fundamental agreement among the reformers proved a mistake. Even the personal friendships which developed in the many conferences could not overcome the obstacles to unity. Zwingli is reported to have shed tears at Marburg, and Luther was willing to meet with Bucer even though he abused him in print. A peace party never really developed, though Strassburg and Hesse supported

Bucer in his efforts. The sense of knowing God's plan for the universe was too strong in the reformers to allow concessions in theology. Hastings Eels has summarized the reasons for Bucer's failure: 1) Lutheranism and Zwinglianism were fundamentally opposed on the question of the relation of faith to reason; 2) unity was impossible because there was no standard for measuring the truth of theological opinion, and those who worked for unity either had to become a third party and create still more disunity or they had to choose sides. At Wittenberg, Bucer chose the side of Martin Luther.

These attempts at conciliation did not mean the advocacy of the principle of toleration by any of the parties involved. Even Bucer believed in strict church discipline. Yet there was at least one voice raised which sought to obtain religious harmony by tolerating different beliefs. Sebastian Castellio had been a school teacher in Geneva, but had been expelled for differing with Calvin on theology. He had fled to Basel, and there the news of the burning of Servetus reached him. Castellio expounded his views in *De Haereticis* (1554), advocating toleration instead of the arbitrary imposition of theological conformity which led to the burning of heretics. How can we retain the name of Christian if we do not imitate Christ's clemency and mercy? Faith should be free because it resides not in the body, but in the heart, which cannot be reached by the swords of princes.

Castellio reduced Christian dogma to an absolute minimum. We should believe that God is the source of all good and that Christ redeems fallen and sinful men. But, "we need not worry whether the body of Christ is in heaven, whether God has created some to be damned, others to be saved, how Christ descended into hell, and the like. On these points, each may be left to his own opinion and to the revelation of the Saviour." Nevertheless, Castellio held that even unbelievers who denied these principles could not be killed. At the most they may be banished, for the sins of the heart are punished by God and not by men. The prophets, apostles, and even Christ, were once held to be seditious blasphemers, yet they came not to destroy but to fulfill. Castellio summed up his views by asserting that the better a man knows the truth, the less he is inclined to condemn others, and he cited the examples of Christ and His Apostles to prove his point. Here Christian humility led to toleration.

In answer to Castellio, Theodore Béza justified persecution. If we were to imitate the clemency of Christ, could any civil order be observed? Could a thief be hanged? If conscience were inviolable, what was to happen to a murderer who committed homicide for the sake of some personal revelation? Castellio's program would abolish ecclesiastical discipline and lead to the disintegration of the Church. The idea of toleration collided with the reformers' attempts to keep order and to tame the religious individualism which the Reformation released. They wanted to prevent the destruction of stability threatened by the "enthusiasts" or the German peasants. Their fear was not unjustified if we contemplate what actually happened when the barriers of ecclesiastical discipline were destroyed by the English Revolution (1640–1660). Then "opinions monstrous and prodigious started up every day and were broached with impunity in public and private, and multitudes were led astray." Some wanted to implement their personal revelations through an equalitarian political and economic program, and others believed themselves above all moral laws because they were of the elect. Such chaos the reformers wanted to avoid, and they were generally successful in preventing it. In this aim they were sustained by their sense of assurance in the truth, even if this meant the persecution of heretics or the prolonging of Protestant disunity through uncompromising attitudes.

C H A P T E R . . . 5

The Long View

By the end of the sixteenth century both Lutheranism and Calvinism were revolutionary movements which had run their course. The Lutheran Reformation had begun with the "pure" word of Scripture, but now, in an effort to prevent new heresy, Scripture was in danger of being replaced by officially enforced confessions of the faith. The Book of Concord (1580) became binding for two thirds of German Protestantism. It included Luther's Catechism, the Confession of Augsburg, and the articles of the League of Schmalkalden. Contemporaries called the book a "pope made out of paper," and it was indeed the Lutheran counterpart to the decrees of the Council of Trent. Luther himself became sanctified as the "last Elias." Everywhere there were attempts to define religious faith and to enforce the definitions. Calvinism went through a similar evolution. Theodor Béza, Calvin's successor at Geneva, stressed the religious aristocracy of preachers. A series of confessions of faith were enforced: the Gallicana

(1559), Scoticana (1560), and the Heidelberg Catechism (1563). Finally the Synod of Dort (1618), an assembly of Calvinists drawn from many different lands, reaffirmed Calvinist orthodoxy and especially predestination, which had been challenged continuously since Calvin's own lifetime.

The uncompromising attitudes of the reformers led to a rigid orthodoxy of which a man like Luther would have disapproved. He had always opposed the regulation of belief in contrast to the regulation of church organization. But the distinction was too finely made and confessions of faith triumphed in the Lutheran as well as in the Calvinist world. The Anglican Church followed the same pattern. It seemed as if free religious expression had retreated into the hymn which was free from the confines of the letter of faith. Yet, there were attempts at a new stress on the piety of the heart. Johann Arndt (1555–1621) made such an attempt for Lutheranism, and though because of this he was driven from ecclesiastical office, his ideas were to bear fruit. Similarly, Calvinism saw an attempt to revive such piety coupled with a renewed attack on predestination. In such a situation millenarianism came to the fore once more. It was farthest removed from orthodoxy and rejected any kind of visible church organization.

The fact was that orthodoxy could not be maintained over the long run. By the seventeenth century, a "second Reformation" was in the making which stressed a "piety of the heart" and which generated that pietism characteristic of the seventeenth and eighteenth centuries. Moreover, the great age of the radical sects was dawning, especially in England. Quakers, Baptists, and Congregationalists all managed to establish themselves on a sure footing and to shed their "enthusiasm"—their millenarian origins. At the same time the Catholic Church was also having another reformation centered also on piety with saints like Francis de Sales and St. Vincent de Paul. The new dynamic injected into religious life by the Reformation would not remain

quiescent. In this manner religious unity was gone
forever, but it took a stiff battle with the newly established Protestant orthodoxies to accomplish this end.
Only by the middle of the seventeenth century does
a situation pertain in which men could arrive at a
great variety of religious expression and have some
hope of being allowed to follow their own consciences.
This was a long-range rather than short-range result
of the Reformation.

The Reformation produced another intellectual
change which is of equal importance for the future.
Skepticism toward papal power and the Catholic system of thought could be transferred to all forms of
Christianity. For, from one point of view, what Luther
had done was to throw into the market place the discussion of what constitutes a proper standard of
religious knowledge. Moreover, the criterion of faith
which the reformers stressed was whether one had
been chosen by that inner persuasion which enabled
one to examine Scripture and to recognize the truths
therein. Such individualism could lead toward a non-
dogmatic pietism, but it also made it easy for skepticism
to enter religious belief. Erasmus had already ad-
vanced a skeptical attitude toward all belief except a
basic piety: man can never totally understand and
judge the complex superstructure of Christian belief.
Before the Reformation men had tried to fuse Christianity and life, for they then seemed rent asunder.
Now the contrary was happening. The good life was
based upon a simple piety, all the rest was a matter
for theologians imprisoned in their own orthodoxy.
Renaissance ideas were instrumental in this new development, especially Platonism, which tied man and
the universe directly to God and which led to a
pantheism where there was little room for Christ and
none for an organized Church. Moreover, in opposition
to orthodoxy an increasingly important distinction was
made between fundamental and nonfundamental
creeds. This also could lead toward an acceptance of

TEMPLE DE LYON NOMME PARADIS.

A Calvinist Congregation in Lyons During the Reformation.
(Bibliothèque Publique et Universitaire, Genève)

God alone and a rejection of all theology as irrelevant and misleading.

Skepticism toward the Church points ahead to the Enlightenment of the eighteenth century and the belief in God alone (deism). It is correct, however, to see this, in part, as another long-range consequence of the Reformation. Skepticism was certainly furthered by doubts about accepted standards of religious knowledge. Moreover, it received definition in its battles against the revived orthodoxies after the Reformation by calling for a return to "essentials." But it saw these not in Christ-centered terms but instead in a virtuous life within a pantheistic universe into which theology could not intrude.

Both these long-range consequences of the Reformation were revolutionary, pushing Europe into the modern age at a greatly accelerated pace. They required religious diversity, which, in turn, would make it impossible for authority to enforce that religious conformity which everyone, Catholic or Protestant, had hitherto desired. At the same time the secularization of European thought proceeded with added speed. When, some three hundred years later, governments would again try to enforce ideological conformity upon their subjects, it would be done on behalf of a purely secular, non-Christian ideology. Here, an exception must be made for Catholic countries that had a continuity of an established Church, but even there church dominance became a matter of political influence rather than an attempt at enforcing a common faith. England with its Established Church is in that same category. Religious dissent was no longer treason as the rulers before and during the Reformation had regarded it.

But what of the social consequences of the religious upheaval? Such factors had been a part of the basic causes of the Reformation and had accompanied its course. The Reformation was not social in intent, as far as the reformers themselves were concerned, but it was in effect. The territorial rulers were strengthened, and the lower class and bourgeoisie had asserted themselves. This was bound to have an impact. The reformers had envisaged a patriarchal Christian community in which the rulers cared for the poor and prevented economic excesses. One of the very first acts of a reformer who had conquered a town was to insure provision for the poor. Monastic charity ended with the abolition of monastic houses, but neither Luther nor his successors failed to provide for the needs the Church had filled. By making the care of the poor a public responsibility rather than a charity, they took an important step forward. The great poor law legislation in Elizabethan England was in accordance with this move, but other cities and rulers had already done so on the Continent.

The idea of the community involved the responsibility of the citizens for each other in the name of Christian brotherly love, and this responsibility included the poor and the sick. Former monasteries became in parts of Europe, like Hesse, hospitals and asylums. It was a consequence of the Reformation that the State got a new social task and that poverty was lifted from the realm of charity to that of a social problem that was the responsibility of the community to meet. This community was a hierarchical one and the reformers did not envisage anything like democratic elections. The ruler was a true *pater patriae;* his task involved a social responsibility for all of his subjects.

If the reformers furthered the bourgeois in any special manner, this was only indirectly and unconsciously. As they endowed the social mission of the state with a religious purpose, they also endowed all professions with a religious task. No part of life could remain outside of Christian concerns. The Reformation, after all, tried to close the fissure between life and the Church that existed in late medieval Europe. Thus, doing one's duty to one's profession was a Christian command, a contribution to the Christian community. Added stature was given in this way to the bourgeois pursuits of commerce, trade, and law. They were as inherently good as the formerly admired noble warrior or ruler. This did give the bourgeoisie a new status and a new spur to action. They did their daily work not only for profit but also according to a divine command of Christian duty. Yet neither for Luther nor for Calvin did this mean unrestrained economic activity. The idea of the community, the concept of social duty toward the less fortunate, was always present.

Permissiveness toward usury is an important test of how much Luther or Calvin put the capitalist quest of the bourgeoisie above other considerations. Luther is usually described as an economic conservative. This is not entirely true. But he was disturbed about the weight of debts which encumbered much of German property, and while allowing some interest to be taken, he was primarily concerned with protecting the debtor. For him this was a social rather than an economic problem, and it was for this reason that he called upon governments to enforce a just price based upon the daily wages of a laborer. What was revolutionary in Calvin's view of usury was that he applied the same logical mind to economic problems as he did to the construction of his faith. Calvin came to believe that money, far from being sterile (as traditional thought had it), was just as much given by God for the use of man as the products of nature. He could therefore recognize the importance of taking interest for the advancement of the economy, not just as an evil custom which must be checked at all times.

The point about Calvin's greater leniency toward usury is not that he allowed it to operate unchecked (he did not) but that he regarded it in connection with the economics of the community as a whole. Individuals were forbidden to take excessive usury and debtors were protected, but if the interests of the community as a whole were involved, this put a different light on the problem. Then usury could have greater play. His criterion for the taking of interest was, then, the good of the community which might allow it and the protection of the poor and the consumer who must never be victimized by it. The relationship between the Reformation and the development of capitalism is therefore a complex one, and not until the next century do we get the equation of wealth with election. Yet once the idea of profession, of vocation, had been given religious stature, it was not difficult to see religious merit in professional success. Moreover, Calvin's idea of usury could be warped through a belief that the best interests of the whole community are served by a heightened urge for wealth and the prohibitions he laid down could be forgotten. Are the poor not those who have failed in their profession? Thus they must have been rejected by God just as those who succeed must be of the elect. Under such an impulse the idea of the community in which the reformers had believed tended to become meaningless and social duty could be shirked in the name of an equation between wealth and election. Who could care for the reprobate exemplified by the poor?

This attitude was a long-range consequence of the Reformation, however much it transformed the original thought of the reformers themselves. It did not create capitalism, but it gave to the accelerated pace of modern capitalism a religious rationale and certainly a moral impetus. But this is only one side of the coin; the idea of social duty as a religious command also remained alive. Rulers from now on did think of poverty and of economic endeavor as public matters in which the state must have an interest, as the "father" of the community of Christians.

In one other way the bourgeoisie was strengthened as well as the nobility. The confiscation and distribution of the lands of the Church was bound to have social consequences, if the extent of church holdings is remembered. For example, German towns meeting at Speyer (1524) castigated the clerical estate for having goods illegally in their possession (the Church was supposed to be poor) and called for putting them into "better hands." These hands were, in the first instance, those of the rulers, who were usually in debt or needed money. As a consequence, much of the monastic and church lands were sold, benefiting those men who had made themselves useful to the territorial rulers. Such people included the nobility, or at least that section which had given the ruler support. Thus, in England, Henry VIII strengthened the new Tudor nobility with gifts of monastic land. But in all countries such gifts were made to the bourgeoisie. In every case, families attached to the dynasty were strengthened, and the new bureaucracies laid the foundations for their wealth and status. In opposition to the old feudal families, the more modern-minded servants of the ruler emerged as a strong class which had to be reckoned with.

Moreover, the clergy were downgraded as a class or estate. They were now entirely dependent on the ruler and upon what support he chose to give them. For all intents and purposes the clergy were no longer an independent political or economic force in Protestant Europe. As servants of the State their status declined markedly during the century, the more so as rulers were niggardly with financial support. This was an important change in European class structure for which the Reformation was responsible.

Like other cataclysmic events in history, the Reformation is the beginning rather than the end of an epoch. Religious diversity triumphed over established orthodoxy. Skepticism, evolving out of an intensified questioning of the basis of religious knowledge, led to deism and a secularization of thought. The concept of the Christian community was given a definite social content and goal, while the infusing of man's vocation with a religious purpose strengthened the trend toward economic individualism.

Finally, the distribution of church lands forced a

change in class structure as the old, feudally-oriented aristocracy saw itself challenged by newly acquired wealth. Service to the state was the criterion; the nation-state was further strengthened by the Reformation as a whole. To all these, sometimes contradictory, results must be added the continuing impulse from the thought of the reformers themselves as well as from those who were persecuted as radicals.

Like any important and central event in history the Reformation is not a self-contained island. Much of the medieval past informed its events and the consequences of the Reformation reached far into the future. The Reformation stands, however, as a segment of history which, in a peculiarly dynamic manner, furthered the evolution of man from the medieval to the modern age.

Bibliographical Note

The most useful reference work on the period is the *Shaff-Herzog Encyclopedia of Religous Knowledge*, 12 vols. (1908–), together with the *20th-Century Encyclopedia of Religious Knowledge* (1955). Both can be supplemented by the *Catholic Encyclopedia*, 15 vols. (1907–). The most useful handbook of dates, names and short but pertinent information is Karl Heussi, *Kompendium Der Kirchengeschichte* (11th edition, 1957). For the social and economic aspects of the age see the *Encyclopedia of Social Sciences*, 15 vols. (1944). For general bibliography there is Roland H. Bainton, *Bibliography of the Continental Reformation: Materials Available in English* (1935), as well as a useful study by Wilhelm Pauck, "The Historiography of the German Reformation during the Past Twenty Years," *Church History*, IX (1940), 305–340.

The latest general work on the Reformation is H. G. Koenigsberger and George L. Mosse, *Europe in the Sixteenth Century* (1968), which contains full bibliographies. There are also Harold Grimm, *The Reformation Era* (1954), with an excellent list of further readings, and Roland H. Bainton, *The Reformation of the Sixteenth Century* (1952). E. Harris Harbison, *The Age of the Reformation* (1955), is a good summary emphasizing the interplay of churches, states, and classes. *The New Cambridge Modern History*, II, "The Reformation" (1958), contains first-rate interpretations of nearly every aspect of the age. Lewis Spitz, *The Religious Renaissance of the German Humanists* (1963), summarizes in excellent fashion the latest research on this topic. Martin Luther has been the subject of a study by Roland H. Bainton, *Here I Stand* (1950), both scholarly and readable. Ernest G. Schwiebert, *Luther and His Times* (1952), is of special importance for Luther's Wittenberg background as well as for the dissemination of the Reformation. Erik Erikson, *Young Man Luther* (1958), applies psychological insight in a meaningful manner. George W. Forel, *Faith Active in Love*

Albert Hyma's *Luther's Theological Development from Erfurt to Augsburg* (1928) contains useful excerpts from the reformer's writings. Gerald Strauss, *Nuremberg in the Sixteenth Century* (1966), is an important case study in the social structure and religious change within this important city.

Hajo Holborn, *Ulrich von Hutten and the German Reformation* (1937), is the most authoritative book on that figure, while Clyde Manschreck, *Melanchthon, The Quiet Reformer* (1958), is a good biography of that Humanist. There are two excellent biographies of Emperor Charles V: Karl Brandi, *Emperor Charles V* (1933), and Roger Bigelow Merriman's well-written *Rise of the Spanish Empire,* III (1925).

The only major work on Bucer in English is Hastings Eels, *Martin Bucer* (1931). Eels has sketched Bucer's peacemaking activities in "The Failure of Church Unification Efforts during the German Reformation," *Archiv fuer Reformationsgeschichte* (1951), 160–173. There is also great paucity of works on Ulrich Zwingli in English. The best is Oskar Farner, *Zwingli the Reformer* (1952).

John T. McNeill has written a bibliography, "Thirty Years of Calvin Study," *Church History,* XVII (1948), 207–240; XVIII (1949), 241. The best summary of modern Calvin scholarship in book form is François Wendel, *Calvin, The Origin and Development of His Religious Thought* (1963). There are many Calvin biographies of which Quirinus Breen, *John Calvin: A Study in French Humanism* (1931), and J. McKinnon, *Calvin and the Reformation* (1936), are useful. John T. McNeill, *The History and Character of Calvinism* (1954), traces the movement to modern times. Calvin's *Institutes* are available in a *Compendium* edited by Hugh Kerr (1939) as well as in a two-volume edition (1949). George L. Mosse, *Calvinism, Authoritarian or Democratic?* (1957), collects some sources for Calvinist political thought. William Monter, *Calvin's Geneva* (1967), is a good and readable study.

A. G. Dickens, *The English Reformation* (1964), is the authoritative work on that subject. T. M. Parker, *The English*

Reformation to 1558 (1950), is a model of condensation and ripe scholarship. F. M. Powicke, *The Reformation in England* (1941), is a good summary, stressing political and legal factors rather than theology. G. Constant, *The Reformation in England*, 2 vols. (1934, 1941), is a well-balanced analysis by a Catholic historian covering the reigns of Henry VIII and Edward VI. E. G. Rupp, *Studies on the Making of the English Protestant Tradition* (1947), provides a stimulating discussion of the early stages of English reform. A. G. Dickens, *Lollards and Protestants in the Diocese of York, 1509–1558* (1959), is of more than regional importance. Garrett Mattingly, *Catherine of Aragon* (1941), combines readability and scholarship.

C. H. Garrett, *The Marian Exiles* (1938), treats that important group of men, while M. M. Knappen, *Tudor Puritanism* (1939), is the standard work on that subject. Michael Walzer, *The Revolution of the Saints* (1965), is an immensely stimulating discussion of puritanism. John F. H. New, *Anglican and Puritan* (1964), admirably shows the differences between the two. W. K. Jordan, *The Development of Religious Toleration in England*, 3 vols. (1932–1938), gives a thorough analysis of religious trends; the first volume goes to the end of Elizabeth's reign. W. H. Frere, *The English Church in the Reign of Queen Elizabeth and James I* (1904), is still a reliable guide.

On the Catholic Reformation, Pierre Janelle, *The Catholic Reformation* (1949), is a standard work. W. Schenck, *Reginald Pole* (1950), and Paul van Dyke, *Ignatius Loyola* (1926), are first-rate biographies. H. Jedin, *History of the Council of Trent,* 2 vols. (1957–1961), is the standard work on the subject. His small *Kleine Konziliengeschichte* (1959), summarizes his vast researches. Roland H. Bainton is the author of *The Travail of Religious Liberty* (1951), which includes essays on Castellio, Calvin, and Occhino. The same author has also edited and translated Sebastian Castellio, *Concerning Heretics* (1935).

For Bucer's political thought and its influence upon Calvin, see Hans Baron's "Calvinist Republicanism and Its Historical Roots," *Church History* (1939), 30–42. This essay has accepted

Baron's important conclusions. Of great significance for the position of Strassburg is his "Religion and Politics in the German Imperial Cities During the Reformation," *English Historical Review* (July–October, 1937). F. L. Carsten, *Princes and Parliaments in Germany* (1959), is a stimulating and important account of the German scene which changes many older interpretations.

The best discussion of Anabaptist thought is Franklin H. Littell, *The Anabaptist View of the Church* (1958). An important discussion of radicalism centering upon the social factors is Norman Cohn, *The Pursuit of the Millennium* (1957). Ernst Bloch's interesting and controversial *Thomas Muentzer als Theologe der Revolution* (1921), is the only book on the subject. Harold Bender has written the useful study *Conrad Grebel* (1950). George H. Williams, *The Radical Reformation* (1962), is the major work on sixteenth century nonconformist groups. Roland H. Bainton's *Hunted Heretic* (1953), provides a most readable account of Servetus. Richard H. Popkin, *The History of Scepticism from Erasmus to Descartes* (1960), is the best and most authoritative work on that subject. The first chapter is on the "intellectual crisis of the reformation."

On the economic side R. H. Tawney, *Religion and the Rise of Capitalism* (1926), is still the classic, while André Biéler, *La Pensée Economique et Sociale de Calvin* (1959), is the most thorough discussion of the subject to date.

For the evolution of the Reformation into the next century see George L. Mosse, "Changes in Religious Thought," in the *New Cambridge Modern History*, Vol. IV (1970), and Karl Müller, *Kirchengeschichte*, Vol. II/2 (1923), which can be used as a handbook. The best book of pictures and reproductions of Reformation documents is Julius von Pflungk-Hartung, *im Morgenrot der Reformation* (1912). It does not, however, include Calvin or the radicals.

Index

Note: Bold figures denote the main entries. Dates for rulers and popes are given according to their period of rule.